The Book On

Women (for Men)

The Truth About Women and the Myths That
Divide Us

The Book On Series

Jordan Ashford

Published by The Book On Publishing, 2025.

First edition. October 28, 2025

Website: https://thebookon.ca

Substack:
https://thebookonpublishing.substack.com/

The Book On Women (for Men): The Truth About Women and the Myths That Divide Us

First edition. October 28, 2025

Copyright © 2025 The Book On Publishing

ISBN: 978-1-997909-44-6

Written by Jordan Ashford

Other Books in The Book On Series

Table of Contents

Chapter 1: Understanding Women: A New Perspective

Most men approach understanding women the way they might approach learning a new language from a phrasebook—memorizing a few key expressions, hoping context will fill in the gaps, and growing frustrated when the conversation inevitably breaks down. They collect advice like trading cards: maintain eye contact but not too much, be confident but not arrogant, show interest but play it cool. The result is a patchwork of contradictory instructions that treat women as puzzles to be solved rather than people to be understood. This approach fails not because men lack intelligence or good intentions, but because it operates from a fundamentally flawed premise: that women are variations of men who simply need the right code cracked. The truth is far more complex and, ultimately, far more liberating. Women are not running a slightly modified version of male psychology with a few additional features and occasional bugs. They are running an entirely different operating system, shaped by distinct developmental experiences, social conditioning, neurological patterns, and survival strategies that have evolved over lifetimes spent navigating a world that rewards their silence and punishes their assertiveness. Understanding this is not about memorizing new rules or adopting better tactics. It is about recognizing that everything you thought you knew about how humans work might only describe half the human experience. This half was allowed to be default, normal, and universal.

The invisibility of this separate operating system creates a peculiar paradox: women are simultaneously everywhere and nowhere in male consciousness. Men grow up surrounded by women—mothers, sisters, teachers, friends, partners—yet often reach adulthood with only a superficial understanding of their internal lives. This is not mere oversight. It is the predictable outcome of a social architecture that centers male experience as neutral and universal while rendering female experience as niche, mysterious, or ornamental. Consider how many men can describe in detail what it feels like to be rejected by a woman, to pursue female attention, or to navigate male competition for female approval, yet cannot articulate what it might feel like to be a woman receiving that attention, managing those expectations, or existing as the object rather than the subject of those dynamics. The gap in perspective is not symmetrical. Women are required to understand male psychology as a matter of basic social survival—they must predict male reactions, manage male emotions, and navigate male spaces daily. Men face no equivalent requirement. They can move through the world interacting with women constantly while remaining largely ignorant of the weight women carry, the calculations they make, or the exhaustion that accumulates from being simultaneously visible as bodies and invisible as minds.

This asymmetry extends beyond individual relationships into the very structure of knowledge and expertise. When men think about understanding women, they often turn to other men for guidance— pickup artists, relationship coaches, evolutionary psychologists— who promise to decode female behavior through frameworks built on male assumptions. These systems reduce women to biological imperatives, emotional irrationality, or strategic game-players engaged in a battle of the sexes. What they rarely offer is something far simpler and more radical: the recognition that women's behavior makes perfect sense when viewed from within their own context, constraints, and lived reality. A woman who seems to "change her mind" about interest may not be fickle; she may have detected subtle signs of possessiveness that experience taught her to recognize as danger. A woman who struggles to articulate what she needs may not be playing games; she may have learned through hundreds of small interactions that direct statements of need result in being labeled demanding, high-maintenance, or difficult. A woman who appears emotionally volatile may not be irrational; she may be responding to real patterns of dismissal, gaslighting, and invalidation that men simply do not register because they are not the targets. Reframing female behavior from "confusing" to "contextually rational" requires men to do something uncomfortable: acknowledge that their perspective has been incomplete and their confusion has been a form of privilege.

The Cost of Adaptation

Women spend their entire lives adapting to male comfort, often so seamlessly that both men and women fail to notice the adaptation happening. This is not a conscious conspiracy or a character flaw—it is a survival skill developed early and reinforced constantly through social reward systems that punish female authenticity while rewarding female accommodation. Young girls learn to laugh at jokes that are not funny, to soften their intelligence to avoid intimidating boys, to minimize their space in conversations, and to manage the emotions of others before their own. By adolescence, this adaptation becomes automatic, a background process running constantly to calibrate speech, expression, posture, and presence against an invisible standard that asks, "Will this make him uncomfortable? Will this make me unsafe?" Adult women navigate professional environments where they must be assertive enough to be taken seriously but not so forceful that they are labeled aggressive, competent enough to earn respect but not so competent that they threaten male ego, and friendly enough to be likable but not so friendly that their boundaries are ignored. They manage romantic relationships where they are expected to provide emotional support, sexual availability, domestic labor, and social coordination while also maintaining careers, friendships, and their own psychological well-being. They do all of this while being told that their struggles are the result of biological differences, personal choices, or their own emotional inadequacy rather than a rational response to real constraints.

The invisibility of this adaptation is precisely what makes it so exhausting. Men rarely witness the constant recalibration because women have become experts at making it look effortless. A woman does not announce, "I am now softening my tone to avoid being perceived as bitchy" or "I am laughing at your mediocre joke to maintain social harmony," or "I am pretending not to notice that you interrupted me for the third time because confronting it will make me the problem." These adjustments happen in microseconds, hundreds of times per day, and their cumulative weight is staggering. When women finally express frustration, anger, or exhaustion, men often respond with genuine confusion because they never saw the labor that preceded the breaking point. From the male perspective, everything was fine until suddenly it was not—she seemed happy until she snapped, she said yes until she said no, she was engaged until she withdrew. What men miss is the entire invisible spectrum of female communication that preceded those moments: the subtle verbal cues, the body language, the tone shifts, the increasingly direct statements that were dismissed or ignored until the only option left was volume or exit.

This dynamic creates a feedback loop that reinforces male obliviousness. Because women adapt, men never have to. Because men never have to, they never develop the skills to notice when adaptation is happening. Because they do not see, they cannot appreciate the effort or recognize when they are demanding too much. And because they cannot realize it, women must continue adapting—except now with the added burden of knowing their partners do not see what they are doing or understand what it costs. This is not about individual men being callous or deliberately exploitative. Most men genuinely believe they are in egalitarian partnerships where both people contribute equally and both people's needs matter equally. What they fail to see is that the apparent equality is maintained through disproportionate female labor—emotional, social, domestic, and psychological. Women do the work of making relationships function smoothly, managing social calendars, remembering birthdays, initiating difficult conversations, noticing when something is wrong, and then they are told they are naturally better at these things, as if the skill appeared without cultivation and the cultivation did not come at tremendous personal cost.

The Neuroscience of Misunderstanding

Recent neuroscience research reveals that male and female brains are far more similar than different. Yet, the small differences that do exist have been weaponized to justify vast disparities in treatment and expectation. For decades, popular psychology claimed that men were from one planet and women from another, that male brains were wired for logic and female brains for emotion, that these differences were immutable and explained everything from communication styles to career choices. The reality emerging from sophisticated brain imaging and longitudinal studies tells a different story: human brains are remarkably plastic, shaped profoundly by experience and environment, and the differences we observe between men and women are often the result of socialization rather than biological destiny. When researchers control for cultural factors and life experiences, many supposed sex differences shrink dramatically or disappear entirely. The differences that remain tend to be matters of degree rather than kind, with enormous overlap between male and female populations and far greater variation within each sex than between them.

Where neuroscience does reveal meaningful distinctions, they rarely align with stereotypes. Women show somewhat enhanced activity in brain regions associated with memory consolidation and emotional processing, but this does not mean they are slaves to emotion—it means they may have a superior ability to integrate emotional information with other data when making decisions, a cognitive advantage rather than a liability. Men show somewhat greater activity in regions associated with spatial processing, but this does not make them inherently better at mathematics or engineering—it makes them slightly more likely to approach certain problems through spatial metaphors, a difference in strategy rather than capability. The notion that women are naturally more empathetic while men are naturally more rational falls apart under scrutiny. Both empathy and logical thinking engage similar neural networks in both sexes, and performance on empathy tasks is heavily influenced by motivation and context. When men are told that empathy is a valuable leadership skill, their performance improves dramatically. When women are told that a spatial task measures something other than math ability, their stereotype threat decreases and their performance rises. These findings point to an uncomfortable truth: much of what we attribute to hardwired biological differences is actually the result of self-fulfilling prophecies, where expectations shape development and then we mistake the outcome for the cause.

The implications for male-female relationships are profound. When men assume that women are naturally more emotional, they stop taking women's emotions seriously as data about reality. A woman's anger becomes "she's being emotional" rather than "I did something worth being angry about." A woman's anxiety becomes "she's overreacting" rather than "she's perceiving risks I'm not seeing." This dismissal is not merely insulting—it is epistemologically destructive, severing men from a crucial source of information about how their behavior impacts others and about aspects of reality that their own socialization has trained them not to perceive. Women, meanwhile, are told that their emotional responses are evidence of cognitive weakness rather than sophisticated social intelligence. The ability to read subtle shifts in tone, to detect incongruence between words and body language, to sense when someone is withholding information or managing hidden resentment—these are advanced cognitive skills developed through years of necessity. Women hone these abilities because their safety and success depend on accurately assessing interpersonal dynamics in environments where power is distributed unequally. When men dismiss these perceptions as "women's intuition" or "paranoia," they are not rejecting mysticism—they are rejecting expertise they never needed to develop and therefore do not recognize as real.

Emotional Labor and the Invisible Infrastructure

The concept of emotional labor—originally coined to describe the work of managing one's own emotions to create appropriate atmospheres in professional settings—has been expanded to explain the disproportionate burden women carry in monitoring, managing, and maintaining the emotional climate of relationships. This labor is invisible precisely because it is preemptive and preventative. It is the mental load of remembering that your partner's mother's birthday is approaching and coordinating a gift and phone call. It is the diplomatic work of smoothing over your partner's social awkwardness at gatherings without making him feel criticized. It is the vigilance of tracking his moods and adjusting your approach accordingly, bringing up difficult topics when he seems receptive and shelving them when he looks stressed. It is the thankless task of being the relationship's emotional maintenance worker, identifying problems early, initiating repairs, and ensuring that the machinery runs smoothly enough that no one notices it is machinery at all.

Men often protest that they never asked for this labor, that they would be fine without it, that women are creating unnecessary work. This misses the point entirely. The labor is unnecessary only if you are willing to accept the consequences of its absence: missed birthdays and damaged family relationships, social isolation and awkward gatherings, unaddressed resentments that calcify into contempt, and emotional illiteracy that leaves both partners lonely in proximity. Women perform this work not because they are naturally better at it or because they enjoy it, but because the alternative—living in the emotional squalor that results when no one does it—is intolerable. When women stop performing emotional labor, relationships do not become more equitable; they collapse. This is not because the labor was really necessary all along; it is because men have not developed the skills or awareness to perform their share, having been excused from it their entire lives.

The gender asymmetry in emotional labor has measurable consequences. Research on heterosexual couples shows that women provide far more emotional support to their partners than they receive in return, that women are more likely to notice when their partners are upset and less likely to have their own distress noticed, and that women's emotional well-being suffers more from relationship problems. In contrast, men's emotional well-being depends heavily on having a female partner to outsource emotional processing to. Divorced men remarry faster and report more severe emotional consequences from being single than divorced women do, not because women are naturally more self-sufficient, but because single men are losing their primary source of emotional support and regulation. In contrast, single women are being released from an exhausting second shift of unpaid care work. The pattern is clear: many men outsource major portions of their emotional lives to female partners without recognizing they are doing so, then experience the loss of that support as devastating when relationships end, while remaining unable to name what they lost or reproduce it on their own.

Dismantling the Myths That Keep Men Confused

Several pervasive myths distort male understanding of women so thoroughly that they must be named and demolished before progress can occur. The first is the myth of female irrationality: the idea that women are governed by emotion in ways that render them inconsistent, unpredictable, or cognitively unreliable. This myth persists despite overwhelming evidence that women make excellent decisions, perform equally to men on virtually all measures of reasoning and judgment, and frequently outperform men in situations requiring consideration of multiple variables and long-term consequences. What men label as emotional irrationality is usually one of two things: either rational responses to contexts men do not understand or recognize, or the visible manifestation of exhaustion from performing invisible labor that men benefit from but do not see. When a woman becomes upset that her partner forgot their anniversary, she is not being irrational—she is responding to evidence that she is investing more attention and care into the relationship than she is receiving. When a woman changes plans last-minute, she is not being flighty—she is often accommodating new information, managing competing demands, or correcting for previous assumptions that proved incorrect. The myth of irrationality is ultimately a failure of empathy and imagination, an inability to consider that behavior that appears confusing from the outside might be perfectly logical from within.

The second myth is that of female manipulation: the notion that women are inherently strategic, withholding, and prone to testing or game-playing in relationships. This myth is particularly insidious because it reframes women's legitimate boundaries and communication patterns as hostile acts. When a woman does not immediately text back, she is "playing hard to get" rather than simply being busy. When she declines sex, she is "withholding" rather than not wanting sex at that moment. When she expresses hurt over something that seems trivial to her partner, she is "making a big deal out of nothing" rather than communicating about something that carries weight in her experience. The manipulation myth allows men to avoid accountability by recasting their partners' needs and boundaries as strategic maneuvers in a game rather than sincere expressions of internal experience. It also creates a double bind: when women communicate indirectly to soften the impact of difficult messages, they are accused of being unclear; when they speak directly, they are accused of being harsh or demanding. The only way to win is not to have needs at all—which is, of course, the unstated goal of the manipulation myth.

The third myth is that understanding women requires men to abandon their masculinity, become more feminine, or sacrifice their own needs and authenticity. This myth treats empathy as emasculating and emotional literacy as weakness, ensuring that men who attempt to develop these capacities face social punishment from other men and internal anxiety about their identity. The reality is that understanding women requires no sacrifice of masculinity—unless your definition of masculinity requires ignorance, emotional stunting, and interpersonal incompetence. Genuine strength includes the capacity to sit with discomfort, to acknowledge mistakes, and to change course when evidence shows you are wrong. Genuine confidence consists of the security to listen to criticism without becoming defensive, to admit what you do not know without feeling diminished. The men who protest most loudly that empathy training is feminization are often those most trapped in a version of masculinity so fragile that it cannot tolerate growth, vulnerability, or the recognition that other people's experiences might be as real and valid as their own.

The Path Forward: Reconstructing Understanding

Moving beyond these myths and developing a genuine understanding requires men to undertake several challenging shifts in perspective. The first is epistemic humility: the recognition that your experience is not universal and that areas where you feel confused might reflect your own ignorance rather than others' incomprehensibility. When women's behavior confuses you, the appropriate first response is not "women are confusing" but rather "I am missing context." This shift transforms confusion from a statement about women into a statement about your own knowledge gaps, which immediately makes it solvable. You cannot fix women being confusing, but you can address your own lack of understanding through curiosity, attention, and the willingness to be wrong. Epistemic humility also means recognizing that your intentions do not determine your impact. Men often defend themselves by pointing to good intentions: "I didn't mean to hurt you," "I was trying to help," "I thought I was being nice." Good intentions matter, but they do not erase harm or excuse you from learning why your approach failed. Women do not care primarily about your intentions; they care about your impact and your willingness to adjust behavior based on outcomes.

The second shift is from transactional to relational thinking. Many men approach relationships with women through an exchange framework: I did X, so she should do Y; I gave her compliments, so she should give me affection; I listened to her problem, so she should solve mine. This framework reduces human interaction to commerce and generates constant disappointment because other people do not exist to fulfill bargains you invented in your head. Relational thinking recognizes that people are ends in themselves, not means to your ends, and that their responses emerge from their own complex histories, needs, and contexts rather than from equations you can balance. This shift eliminates the entitled resentment that poisons many male-female relationships—the sense that women "owe" men attention, affection, or sex in exchange for basic decent behavior. It replaces scorekeeping with genuine interest in the other person's experience and invests in relationship quality for its own sake rather than as a strategy to extract specific outcomes.

The third shift is from defensiveness to accountability. When women tell you that something you did hurt them, annoyed them, or made them uncomfortable, the defensive response is to explain why they are wrong to feel that way, why your actions were justified, or why they are being too sensitive. The accountable response is to recognize that impact matters regardless of intent, to apologize for the harm caused, and to inquire about what a different approach would work better. Defensiveness prioritizes protecting your self-image over improving your behavior. It values being seen as good more than actually doing good. Accountability accepts that you will make mistakes, that making mistakes does not mean you are irredeemably terrible, and that the measure of character is what you do after being informed of your mistakes. Most women are not asking for perfection; they are asking for partners who can hear criticism without collapsing into self-pity or counterattacking, who can sit with the discomfort of being wrong, and who demonstrate through changed behavior that they value the relationship more than they value being right.

Understanding women is not a parlor trick or a skill you master once and file away. It is an ongoing practice of attention, curiosity, and humility. It requires recognizing that women have been studying men their entire lives as a matter of survival, while men have had the luxury of not reciprocating. It demands that you become a student of experiences that are not your own, perspectives that challenge your assumptions, and realities that your socialization trained you not to see. Most fundamentally, it asks you to treat women as the authorities on their own experiences rather than assuming you know better what they think, feel, or need than they do. This is not about self-flagellation or surrendering your own needs. It is about recognizing that genuine partnership requires two people who see each other clearly, and that clarity has been dangerously asymmetrical for far too long. The work of understanding women is actually the work of growing up—moving from a narcissistic worldview where others exist primarily as supporting characters in your story to a mature recognition that you exist in a world of other minds, other truths, and other experiences that are just as real and valid as your own.

Chapter 2: The Myth of Mixed Signals: Communication Without Codes

The notion that women send "mixed signals" is perhaps the most pervasive and convenient myth in male-female communication. It absolves men of the responsibility to listen carefully while casting women as enigmatic creatures who intentionally obscure their meaning. The reality is far less mysterious: what men call mixed signals are usually consistent messages delivered through communication channels men have never been taught to monitor. Women do not encrypt their communication for sport or strategy. They communicate with clarity, but that clarity often exists outside the narrow bandwidth of literal verbal statements that men have been socialized to recognize as the only legitimate form of human expression.

Consider the architecture of typical male communication development. Boys are taught that effective communication means stating facts, presenting arguments, and defending positions. Emotional content is stripped away as inefficient noise. A question is a request for information. A statement is a declaration of fact. Silence indicates nothing noteworthy is happening. This framework produces adults who genuinely believe that if something is not explicitly verbalized, it was not communicated. Meanwhile, girls grow up in social ecosystems that require fluency in context, subtext, tone, timing, and relational dynamics. They learn to interpret the space between words, the shift from "fine" delivered with eye contact versus "fine" delivered while turning away, the difference between laughter that invites connection and laughter that establishes distance. By adulthood, women are operating with sophisticated multi-channel communication systems while men are still checking only one frequency and wondering why they keep missing transmissions.

The accusation of mixed signals typically emerges in predictable scenarios. A woman says she would like to spend more time together, but when her partner suggests plans, she expresses hesitation or proposes alternatives. To him, this is contradictory.

To her, she communicated a desire for more quality time. At the same time, his suggestion failed to address the actual issue—perhaps the plans involve activities she finds exhausting rather than connecting, or the timing conflicts with already-communicated needs for rest, or the proposal itself reveals that he has not retained information she has shared about her preferences. She has not changed her mind; he has simply not heard the qualifiers, context, and conditions she embedded in her initial statement. Another common scenario: a woman mentions feeling stressed about a work situation multiple times over several weeks. Her partner offers solutions each time, which she politely acknowledges before changing the subject. Eventually, she stops mentioning work entirely and becomes withdrawn. He is baffled by her sudden coldness. She attempted to communicate her need for emotional support and non-advisory listening through repeated bids for connection that he consistently converted into problem-solving sessions, thereby demonstrating that he was more invested in fixing than understanding. Her withdrawal is not a mixed signal—it is the predictable result of a clear signal being repeatedly ignored.

The Grammar of Female Communication

Understanding women's communication requires learning what might be called paralinguistic grammar—the rules governing meaning that exists adjacent to and around spoken words. This is not manipulation or indirectness; it is linguistic complexity. Linguists have documented that women use significantly more hedging language, tag questions, and qualifiers not because they are uncertain but because they are managing relational dynamics while conveying information. When a woman says, "I might be wrong, but..." before presenting an objection, she is not expressing doubt about her correctness. She is performing the social labor of softening disagreement to reduce the likelihood that her challenge will be met with defensiveness or dismissal. When she asks, "Don't you think we should consider other options?" she is not seeking affirmation of her uncertainty. She is proposing a different direction while attempting to preserve collaborative decision-making rather than issuing a unilateral veto. Men who interpret these constructions as weakness or indecision are functionally illiterate in the language being spoken.

Tone carries enormous information density in female communication, operating as a parallel data stream that modulates and sometimes reverses the meaning of words. The statement "I am fine" can communicate anywhere from genuine contentment to profound hurt depending on pitch, tempo, volume, and the presence or absence of vocal tension. Men frequently claim they cannot decode these variations, but this is learned helplessness rather than biological inability. Research in acoustic phonetics demonstrates that humans across cultures can accurately identify emotional states from vocal patterns when they are motivated to do so. The issue is not detection capability but interpretive priority. Men have been socialized to treat tonal information as optional metadata rather than essential content, while women have been taught that ignoring tone is a form of social incompetence. When a woman speaks with a tight, elevated pitch and clipped words while saying everything is fine, she is communicating clearly through a channel men have simply chosen not to learn.

Timing constitutes another dimension of meaning that men routinely miss. When something is said, it matters as much as what is said. A woman who brings up a concern immediately when it occurs is signaling that the issue is urgent and requires direct attention. A woman who mentions something in passing days after it happened may be testing whether her partner notices patterns or only responds to a crisis. A woman who raises a topic during a relaxed moment is creating a safe container for difficult conversation, while the same topic introduced during conflict has entirely different implications about escalation and priority. Men who respond only to the content of statements without recognizing the strategic timing of their delivery are missing half the message. Similarly, the choice to say nothing in a moment where speech would be expected is itself a powerful communication act—one that men often fail to register as communication at all, instead experiencing it merely as absence.

The Request System

Women have developed elaborate frameworks for making requests because direct asking has been systematically punished throughout their lives. A woman who states her needs plainly is often labeled demanding, high-maintenance, or selfish—a woman who explains why her request matters may be dismissed as over-explaining or creating drama. A woman who expresses frustration that her needs are unmet is accused of being emotional or unreasonable. Consequently, many women have learned to embed requests within observations, suggestions, or questions—not to be coy, but to avoid the social penalties that attach to female desire expressed without sufficient cushioning. When a woman says, "The kitchen is really messy," she is not providing meteorological data about household conditions. She is making a request that domestic labor be addressed, phrased as a neutral observation to test whether her partner will demonstrate initiative without requiring explicit direction. If he responds, "Yeah, it is," and does nothing, he has failed a communication test he did not know he was taking.

This indirect request structure frustrates men who insist they prefer direct communication, yet the same men often react negatively when women do ask directly. A woman who says, "I need you to do the dishes tonight" may be met with defensiveness about being told what to do, accusations that she is treating him like a child, or resistance framed as concerns about her tone. Her "nagging" is actually the result of repeated attempts at indirect requests that went unheeded, forcing escalation to directness that is then punished for being too direct. The double bind is exquisite: indirect requests are mixed signals, but direct requests are disrespectful demands. The only winning move in this system is for women to ensure that men want to do what women need them to do without ever having to ask—a cognitive and emotional burden that transfers the entire weight of coordination and initiation onto women. In contrast, men get to experience themselves as spontaneous and generous rather than responsive and accountable.

The "hints" that men claim to find incomprehensible are often remarkably straightforward communications that men have learned to ignore because acknowledging them would require action. A woman who mentions multiple times that she feels disconnected, that she misses having conversations like they used to have, that she wishes they could spend an evening without screens—these are not cryptic clues. These are clear statements of need delivered in a non-confrontational register that preserves plausible deniability for the man. He can claim he did not realize it was serious, that she never directly asked for what she wanted, that he thought she was just making conversation. This plausible deniability is precisely the point. Women provide off-ramps and face-saving exits even as they attempt to communicate needs, because experience has taught them that male defensiveness is a more predictable outcome than male responsiveness. When women finally issue ultimatums or explicit demands, men experience this as a sudden escalation. In reality, it is the final resort after dozens or hundreds of "hints" have been systematically dismissed.

The Epistemology of No

One of the most dangerous zones of miscommunication involves consent, boundaries, and refusal. Men have been acculturated in systems where a female "no" is treated as a negotiable opening position rather than a complete sentence. This is not about malice; it is about training. Boys watch movies where persistence overcomes female reluctance, where the romantic hero succeeds by refusing to take no for an answer, and where the eventual yes validates the initial no as merely a test of male determination. They observe fathers negotiating with mothers, wearing down objections through repetition, humor, or strategic timing. They participate in peer cultures where male status accrues to those who can successfully pressure women past initial resistance. By adulthood, many men genuinely do not recognize female refusal as information to be respected but rather as a problem to be solved.

Women, meanwhile, have learned that delivering an unambiguous no carries significant risks. Straightforward refusal can trigger male anger, aggression, or retaliation. It can result in being called a tease, a prude, or worse. It can transform a merely uncomfortable situation into a dangerous one. Consequently, women have developed a repertoire of soft nos: "I am not sure," "Maybe another time," "I do not really feel like it," "I am tired," "I have to get up early," or subject changes that redirect away from unwanted proposals. These are not mixed signals. They are risk-management strategies that allow women to decline while minimizing the chance of a negative male reaction. The problem is that men have been socialized to interpret anything short of "absolutely not under any circumstances" as "keep trying." They genuinely believe they are being respectful by accepting these soft nos at face value while simultaneously working to change the conditions that produced the no, thereby converting it retroactively into a yes.

The "freeze" response further complicates this terrain. Neurobiological research on threat responses reveals that when humans perceive danger but cannot effectively fight or flee, they often enter a dissociative state characterized by physical stillness and psychological absence. This is not consent; it is a trauma response. Yet men frequently interpret female freezing as acquiescence, particularly in sexual contexts. A woman who stops resisting, who becomes quiet and still, who ceases to actively refuse—this is not agreement. This is a nervous system determining that continued resistance is more dangerous than immobility. The absence of no is not the presence of yes, yet men have been taught to fill silence with whatever interpretation serves their goals. Women understand this, which is why they often report feeling that they "let" something happen even when they did not want it— they accurately recognize that their freeze response was misread as permission. Yet, they also know that explaining the neurobiological reality of that moment will likely be met with denial, minimization, or blame.

Context Collapse and the Relationally Blind

Men often fail to recognize that women's communication is context-dependent in ways that male communication typically is not. A woman who enthusiastically agrees to plans with friends may decline similar plans with her partner, not because she is inconsistent, but because the contexts are entirely different. Time with friends may provide the social replenishment and independence she has been craving. At the same time, similar activities with her partner might represent more of the same unbalanced emotional labor that is depleting her. A woman who is sexually adventurous with one partner may be reserved with another, not because she is selectively withholding, but because the first partner created safety, reciprocity, and genuine desire while the second has not. These are not contradictions. They are sophisticated responses to different relational conditions.

The male tendency toward context blindness—treating all situations as informationally equivalent as long as the surface facts match—creates endless confusion. Men compare themselves to other men women have dated, other scenarios where women behaved differently, or hypothetical situations where they believe women should respond in specific ways. "You did this with him, why not with me?" The answer is that "this" never exists in isolation. Every action, every choice, every communication exists within a web of accumulated interactions, demonstrated patterns, and relational trust or lack thereof. Women are not applying arbitrary double standards. They are responding accurately to genuinely different conditions that men cannot perceive because they do not track relational data with the same granularity.

This extends to how women communicate across different relationships. A woman may be direct and assertive with female friends while being accommodating with male colleagues and carefully calibrated with her romantic partner. Men who observe this variation sometimes interpret it as fakeness or manipulation— surely her "real" personality is whichever version serves as baseline, and the others are strategic performance. This interpretation misses that all versions are real; they are adaptive responses to different social ecosystems with different rules, risks, and rewards. Female friends typically operate within frameworks of reciprocal emotional support where directness is valued. Male colleagues exist within professional hierarchies where female assertiveness is punished. Romantic partners carry different types of power and vulnerability. Women are not being inconsistent; they are being intelligently responsive to accurately perceived environmental conditions. Men who demand that women communicate identically across all contexts are essentially demanding that women be relationally incompetent.

The Bid System and Invisible Invitations

Psychologist John Gottman's research on relationship success identified "bids for connection"—small moments where one partner reaches out for attention, affirmation, or engagement. Women make dozens of these bids daily, most of which men fail to recognize as communicative acts requiring response. A woman comments on something she saw, shares a brief story about her day, points out something in the environment, or expresses a fleeting emotion. These are not mere information transfers; they are invitations into shared attention and emotional presence. When men respond with distraction, minimal acknowledgment, or immediate topic shifts, they are rejecting bids they did not realize were being offered. Women interpret this pattern not as innocent obliviousness but as evidence that their partner is not interested in connection, which is accurate. However, the man himself remains unaware that connection opportunities existed.

The accumulation of rejected bids creates what women describe as loneliness within the relationship. A woman can be physically present with her partner, even in conversation, while experiencing profound isolation because none of her bids are landing. She mentions feeling tired, and he asks what is for dinner. She points out something beautiful, and he does not look up from his phone. She expresses worry about a friend, and he offers a solution that closes the topic rather than opening exploration. Each rejection seems trivial, but the cumulative message is devastating: your internal experience does not warrant my attention, your emotional world is not interesting to me, your bids for connection are interruptions rather than opportunities. Men are often shocked when women describe feeling unseen or unheard because, from the male perspective, they are having conversations, spending time together, and coexisting peacefully. What they miss is that coexistence without emotional attunement is not connection—it is parallel isolation.

The tragedy is that women typically signal clearly when their bids are being rejected and when the pattern is becoming unsustainable. They explicitly state that they feel distant, that something is missing, that they need more presence or attention. Men hear these statements as complaints about quantity—she wants more time, more dates, more activities. They attempt to address the complaint by scheduling more time together, only to find that nothing improves. This is because the issue was never quantity; it was the quality of attention and responsiveness to emotional bids. A woman who feels unheard does not need more hours in the same disconnected dynamic. She needs evidence that her internal world matters to her partner, that her emotional expressions are met with genuine interest rather than polite tolerance. When men fail to understand this distinction, they conclude that women are impossible to satisfy, that nothing they do is enough. The reality is that they are solving the wrong problem because they never accurately decoded the initial communication.

The frustration women express about being misunderstood is not about men failing to read minds. It is about men failing to read communications that were actually delivered through multiple channels with increasing clarity until the only option left was to exit. When women say, "I told you this was important to me," they are not misremembering. They are referring to the ten conversations where they raised the topic with varying degrees of directness, the nonverbal communications that signaled distress, the changes in behavior that indicated growing disengagement, and the explicit statements that articulated needs. Men who claim they had no idea their partner was unhappy are not lying; they genuinely did not register the communications. But this ignorance is not proof that communication failed. It is proof that they never learned to receive on the frequencies where transmission occurred.

Chapter 3: Emotional Labor: Beyond Love and Nurture

The term "emotional labor" entered public consciousness as a descriptor of workplace dynamics—the forced cheerfulness of flight attendants, the manufactured empathy of customer service representatives, the professional warmth required of teachers and nurses. Yet this industrial framing obscures the vast, unmeasured economy of emotional work that operates in private life, where women perform sophisticated psychological services that remain invisible precisely because they are expected, unpaid, and naturalized as feminine instinct. Men routinely mistake this labor for personality traits, genetic disposition, or spontaneous expressions of love rather than recognizing it as skilled work that requires time, energy, and deliberate cognitive effort. The result is a fundamental misapprehension of relationship dynamics in which men believe they are participating equally in partnerships while women are working a second shift of psychological maintenance that never appears on any shared calendar or division-of-labor spreadsheet.

The most pernicious aspect of this invisibility is that emotional labor, when performed well, creates the illusion that no work is happening at all. A woman who successfully manages her partner's insecurities produces a man who feels confident and supported without ever realizing his emotional stability requires external scaffolding. A woman who skillfully navigates family politics creates smooth holiday gatherings where conflict never surfaces, leading relatives to believe harmony exists naturally rather than through meticulous diplomatic effort. A woman who carefully times difficult conversations, moderates her tone, and packages criticism in affirmation creates an environment where her partner can receive feedback without becoming defensive, leading him to believe he is simply good at accepting criticism rather than the beneficiary of a sophisticated pedagogical strategy. This paradox— that successful emotional labor renders itself invisible—ensures that men systematically underestimate the work being done and thus never recognize when they should reciprocate or when demands have become unsustainable.

The Architecture of Anticipatory Care

Women do not merely respond to emotional needs as they arise; they operate elaborate predictive models that identify and address psychological requirements before those needs manifest as problems. This anticipatory dimension of emotional labor involves constant environmental scanning, pattern recognition, and proactive intervention that parallels the cognitive work of project managers or air traffic controllers, yet receives none of the professional recognition accorded to such roles. A woman might notice her partner has been working long hours and proactively arrange a low-pressure weekend, not because he requested it but because she modeled his stress trajectory and predicted imminent burnout. She might observe that his mother's birthday is approaching and take initiative on gift selection, card writing, and planning the celebration because she knows from experience that if left unmanaged, the oversight will create family tension that she will ultimately absorb. She might sense that a friend is struggling and reach out before being asked, or notice that a child needs academic support before grades decline, or recognize that a colleague is being undermined in workplace politics and strategize intervention.

This predictive capacity requires maintaining detailed psychological profiles of everyone in a woman's social ecosystem—tracking not merely preferences and schedules but emotional states, interpersonal dynamics, unspoken tensions, and potential flashpoints. Women often describe feeling as though they are running background processes at all times, monitoring multiple relationships simultaneously for signs of distress, disconnection, or emerging conflict. The cognitive load is substantial: it requires holding vast amounts of social information in active memory, continuously updating models based on new behavioral data, and running simulations about how various actions or inactions might cascade through relationship networks. When men claim they "just don't think about" things like thank-you notes, birthday planning, or checking in with distant relatives, they are describing the luxury of not having to run these background processes, not a fundamental cognitive inability. Women think about these things because they have learned through social conditioning and direct consequences that failures in relationship maintenance will be attributed to them, regardless of who technically held responsibility.

The anticipatory nature of this work also means women are managing problems that never occur, preventing conflicts that never materialize, and smoothing interactions that appear effortless to everyone who benefits from them. This creates an impossible accounting challenge: how does one quantify work whose success is measured by the absence of problems? When a man asks what his partner did all day and she struggles to articulate specific accomplishments, the issue is not that she did nothing but that much of what she did was preventing negative outcomes rather than producing visible products. She headed off an argument with his mother by carefully wording a text message, she maintained a friendship by remembering to send a supportive note during a difficult time, she sustained family cohesion by coordinating a gathering that required negotiating six different schedules and dietary restrictions—none of which registers as "work" in frameworks that value only tangible deliverables.

Relational Systems Administration

Beyond managing individual emotional states, women function as administrators of entire relationship ecosystems, maintaining the social infrastructure that allows families, friend groups, and communities to function. This meta-level labor involves tracking relationship histories between multiple parties, translating between different communication styles, mediating conflicts, maintaining institutional memory about traditions and expectations, and ensuring that social connections do not atrophy from neglect. A woman might be simultaneously managing her relationship with her partner, her partner's relationship with his family, her own family relationships, friendships that predate the partnership, couple friendships that require coordination between four people, professional networks, and her children's social ecosystems. Each of these relationship nodes requires active maintenance—remembering birthdays, initiating contact, planning gatherings, sending updates, offering support during crises, and performing the countless small acts of acknowledgment that sustain social bonds.

Men frequently assume these relationship networks maintain themselves or that their persistence reflects natural affinity rather than deliberate cultivation. When a man has a close relationship with his siblings, he often attributes it to family loyalty rather than recognizing that his partner has been the one organizing regular calls, planning holiday visits, and keeping him informed about significant events in his siblings' lives. When couple friendships thrive, men may believe they simply have good friends rather than noticing that their partners are doing the work of coordinating schedules, suggesting activities, and ensuring regular contact. When extended family gatherings happen smoothly, men attend and enjoy them without recognizing the hours of planning, negotiation, and emotional management that preceded the event. This creates a profound asymmetry in which men experience rich social lives as natural phenomena while women understand them as maintained systems requiring constant input.

The systems administration metaphor is precise: like IT professionals who become visible only when systems fail, women's relationship maintenance work becomes apparent only when it stops. When women withdraw this labor—whether through deliberate choice, illness, depression, or sheer exhaustion—men suddenly discover that friendships require effort to maintain, family members need proactive contact, children require educational advocacy, and social calendars do not populate themselves. The shock men experience when these systems collapse reveals how thoroughly they had naturalized women's labor as the default state of reality rather than as ongoing work. The common male complaint that "she just stopped trying" after a breakup or separation often translates more accurately as "the relationship infrastructure I took for granted stopped being maintained, and I have no idea how to operate it myself."

Emotional Translation and Code-Switching

Women perform constant translation work between different emotional languages and communication styles, functioning as interpreters who make interaction possible between parties who would otherwise talk past each other. This translation happens most obviously between men and women—where women learn to decode male communication styles while translating their own meanings into formats men can receive—but extends far beyond gender dynamics. Women translate between generations, helping aging parents and adult children communicate across decades of cultural change. They translate between personality types, assisting direct communicators and indirect communicators to understand each other. They translate between emotional styles, explaining to logical processors what emotionally expressive people need and vice versa. They translate between cultural contexts, navigating ethnic, religious, and class differences within extended families or social groups.

This translation work requires fluency in multiple communication systems simultaneously and the cognitive flexibility to shift between them rapidly as contexts change. A woman might use one communication approach with her partner's emotionally reserved father, another with her own gregarious mother, another with professional colleagues, another with her children's teachers, and another with close friends—adjusting vocabulary, directness, emotional expression, and topic selection to match each audience. She does this not because she lacks authenticity but because she has learned that effective communication requires meeting people within their own frameworks rather than demanding they adapt to hers. The exhaustion comes not merely from the switching itself but from the fact that one direction of translation is socially mandated. At the same time, the reverse is optional: women must learn male communication styles to be taken seriously in professional contexts, yet men face no equivalent pressure to learn female communication patterns.

Beyond linguistic translation, women perform emotional translation—converting feelings into formats that others can process and respond to appropriately. A woman might feel hurt but express disappointment because she has learned her partner shuts down in response to expressions of pain. She might feel angry, but present the same concern because anger from women is routinely dismissed as hysteria, while concern might be heard. She might feel overwhelmed, but describes herself as needing support because admitting to overwhelm could be interpreted as incompetence. This constant emotional code-switching means women rarely get to experience the relief of being fully understood in their native emotional language; instead, they are perpetually translating their internal experiences into dialects that others can parse. Men, meanwhile, are granted the privilege of emotional monolingualism—they can communicate in their natural register and expect others to translate inward rather than taking responsibility for translating outward.

The Weaponization of Incompetence

One of the most corrosive patterns in emotional labor distribution is strategic incompetence—the phenomenon where men claim inability to perform emotional or relational tasks not because they lack capacity but because demonstrated incompetence exempts them from future responsibility. When a man "forgets" important dates repeatedly, plans gifts so inappropriately that his partner must take over, or manages conflicts so badly that he is excluded from future negotiations, these are not random failures of memory or skill. They are, often unconsciously, strategic performances of incompetence that transfer labor back to women while allowing men to avoid accountability. The logic is simple: if he cannot do it well, she will do it instead, and he bears no blame because he "tried his best." This dynamic allows men to benefit from emotional labor while claiming they are constitutionally incapable of providing it, positioning themselves as the beneficiaries of female competence rather than as adults refusing to develop necessary skills.

Women face an impossible bind when confronting strategic incompetence. If they accept it at face value and perform the labor themselves, they enable the incompetence and guarantee it will continue. If they refuse to compensate and allow systems to fail—

missed birthdays, neglected friendships, forgotten appointments—they are blamed for the failure because women are held socially accountable for relationship maintenance regardless of who technically held responsibility. If they attempt to teach or guide their partners through emotional tasks, they are accused of being controlling, nagging, or treating grown men like children. If they express frustration about the unequal distribution, they are told they are creating unnecessary drama over minor issues. Every response carries penalties, which is precisely how strategic incompetence maintains itself: the system is designed to make the cost of challenging it higher than the cost of accepting it.

The cruelty of strategic incompetence lies in its deniability. Because emotional and relational tasks are undervalued and invisible, men can claim they simply have different priorities or standards rather than admitting they are refusing to develop skills. A man might genuinely believe he is "bad at remembering dates" rather than recognizing he has never built the reminder systems or devoted the attention that would make him competent at it. He might truly think he is "not good with people" rather than acknowledging he has never invested in learning social dynamics because women have always managed that domain for him. The incompetence feels authentic to him precisely because he has been allowed to remain incompetent while still enjoying the benefits of others' competence. Women, recognizing the performance, experience a particular kind of gaslighting where their accurate perception of strategic behavior is dismissed as unfair attribution of malicious intent to innocent inability.

The Expectation of Selflessness

Emotional labor carries an expectation of selflessness that does not apply to other forms of work—an assumption that if women expect reciprocity, acknowledgment, or compensation, they are fundamentally misunderstanding the nature of care. Men frequently respond to requests for equitable distribution of emotional labor with hurt or confusion, as though women are attempting to transactionalize love or impose capitalist exchange principles on domains that should remain above such accounting.

This framing positions women who want fairness as emotionally deficient, lacking the natural feminine generosity that would make emotional labor feel like joy rather than a burden. The expectation is that women should provide emotional care as a spontaneous expression of love, requiring no conscious effort and seeking no return. This expectation would be immediately recognized as exploitative if applied to any form of paid labor.

This ideology of selfless femininity serves a clear function: it allows men to continue receiving emotional care while avoiding reciprocal obligation. If emotional labor is love made visible, then keeping score is a betrayal of love itself. If women naturally derive satisfaction from caring for others, then they require no recognition or reciprocation. If nurturing is instinctive rather than skilled, then it neither deserves appreciation nor imposes debt. These narratives allow men to experience themselves as good partners while providing minimal emotional labor themselves—after all, if women enjoy this work and men do not, expecting men to do half would be imposing an unfair burden. The framework is precisely inverted: women's competence at emotional labor is treated as evidence that they should do more of it, while men's incompetence is treated as evidence that they should be excused from it.

Women who resist this expectation face accusations that they are selfish, unloving, or damaged—that a healthy woman would find joy in self-sacrifice and would not experience emotional labor as labor at all. The therapeutic establishment has historically reinforced this narrative, pathologizing women who experience caretaking as burdensome rather than questioning why society distributes caretaking so unequally. Self-help literature aimed at women rarely asks whether they are doing too much emotional labor; instead, it offers strategies for doing emotional labor more efficiently, with better boundaries, or with greater self-care—all of which preserve the fundamental expectation that women will continue serving as primary emotional laborers while simply managing their own exhaustion more effectively. The possibility that men could and should develop equivalent emotional labor capacity is rarely considered as the obvious solution.

The transition to recognizing emotional labor as labor rather than love does not diminish authentic care; it clarifies it. When emotional work is visible, valued, and distributed equitably, the care that remains is more likely to be genuine rather than coerced by gendered expectations. Women who feel their labor is acknowledged and reciprocated have more capacity for spontaneous generosity because they are not operating from a deficit. Men who develop emotional labor skills become better partners, friends, and parents, not because they are performing obligations grudgingly but because they finally have access to the full range of human relational capacity. The resistance to this recognition comes not from men's incapacity for emotional labor but from the comfortable privileges of remaining incompetent— privileges that are only sustainable when women continue accepting responsibility for the emotional architecture that makes all other life possible.

Chapter 4: Neuroscience of Empathy: Bridging Emotional Worlds

The biological architecture of empathy reveals why men and women often experience the same emotional moment from seemingly incompatible vantage points. Contemporary neuroscience has moved beyond simplistic "female brain versus male brain" narratives to illuminate how empathic processing operates through multiple, dissociable neural systems that develop differently based on socialization, threat environment, and relational practice. The most critical finding for understanding male-female dynamics is not that women possess some empathy organ that men lack. Still, that empathic capacity relies on neural networks that require consistent activation to remain efficient. When these networks atrophy from disuse—as they do in men who are socially permitted to outsource emotional awareness—the subjective experience is not "I am choosing not to empathize" but rather "I genuinely do not perceive what you are asking me to perceive." This distinction matters enormously because it reframes male empathy deficits from moral failures into skill atrophy, suggesting that capacity exists but has been allowed to deteriorate through social permission to remain emotionally illiterate.

The default mode network, which activates during rest and supports self-referential thinking and social cognition, shows measurably different connectivity patterns between individuals with high versus low empathic ability. Research using functional magnetic resonance imaging has demonstrated that people who regularly engage in perspective-taking show enhanced connectivity between the medial prefrontal cortex—associated with thinking about mental states—and the posterior cingulate cortex, which integrates emotional and cognitive information. Men who have been socialized to prioritize instrumental problem-solving over relational attunement show weaker connectivity in these pathways, not because testosterone has destroyed the wiring but because decades of not using empathic circuitry have allowed it to become less integrated and less automatically activated. When such men encounter their partners' emotional distress, their brains quite literally do not spontaneously activate the networks that would generate understanding of the other person's subjective experience. They are not refusing empathy; they are experiencing a neural architecture that has been shaped by permission to abdicate emotional responsibility.

The Mirror Neuron Myth and Reality

Popular discussions of empathy have fixated on mirror neurons—brain cells that fire both when we perform an action and when we observe someone else performing that action—as the biological explanation for why we feel what others feel. This narrative is appealing but dangerously incomplete. Mirror neuron systems certainly contribute to empathic resonance. Still, they represent only the most automatic, primitive level of empathic response: the visceral, body-level mimicry that makes us wince when we see someone injured or unconsciously mirror the posture of someone we are speaking with. This motor-level resonance is largely intact in men and does not explain the gender empathy gap. What differs is not the capacity for automatic resonance but the subsequent cognitive elaboration—the deliberate, effortful process of translating visceral resonance into an accurate understanding of another person's subjective experience and then using that understanding to guide behavior.

The anterior insula and anterior cingulate cortex constitute what neuroscientists call the salience network, which determines what information receives conscious attention and emotional significance. Studies tracking eye movements and neural activation patterns reveal that women and men with high trait empathy show earlier and more sustained activation in these regions when viewing faces in distress. In contrast, men with lower trait empathy show delayed activation or activation only when explicitly instructed to empathize. This is not a hardware difference; it is a calibration difference. Men whose social environments have taught them that others' emotional states are not their concern develop salience networks that deprioritize emotional information, filtering it out before it reaches conscious awareness. When a woman tells such a man that she is upset, his brain may register the words without activating the neural systems that would generate an appropriate emotional response, creating the subjective experience of hearing a statement that feels abstract rather than urgent. She experiences herself as communicating something emotionally obvious; he experiences himself as receiving information that seems tangential to whatever practical matter is at hand.

The gap between automatic resonance and cognitive empathy explains why men often fail at empathy in precisely the moments when they report feeling their partners' distress most intensely. A man might genuinely feel his own anxiety spike when his partner is upset—his mirror neurons and emotional contagion systems are functioning normally—but then respond to his own discomfort rather than to her experience. He attempts to shut down the conversation, solve the problem quickly, or minimize the situation, not because he does not care, but because he is reacting to his own distress at witnessing her distress rather than responding to what she actually needs. His empathic response stops at the level of "I feel bad when you feel bad, so I need you to stop feeling bad so I stop feeling bad," never progressing to "What is your subjective experience, and what response from me would honor that experience?" This truncated empathy feels to women like narcissism—he is making her distressed about him—but neurologically it represents failure to move from automatic emotional contagion into deliberate perspective-taking.

Cognitive Load and Empathic Bandwidth

The brain's capacity for empathic processing is not infinite; it operates within metabolic constraints that make empathy more difficult under conditions of stress, cognitive depletion, or competing attentional demands. The prefrontal cortex, which supports the executive functions necessary for perspective-taking and emotional regulation, is among the most metabolically expensive neural regions and among the first to show performance degradation when resources are scarce. Men who are stressed, exhausted, or cognitively depleted show particularly steep declines in empathic accuracy—their ability to correctly identify what others are feeling drops significantly below baseline. Women show similar declines, but the baseline difference means that even depleted women often outperform non-depleted men on empathic tasks because they are starting from a higher level of practiced skill.

This neurometabolic reality has profound implications for relationship dynamics because it means empathy is not simply a matter of caring enough but requires actual cognitive resources that may not be available in moments of high demand. Men who work in cognitively demanding jobs often arrive home with depleted prefrontal resources, meaning their capacity for the effortful processing required for genuine empathy is compromised precisely when their partners need it most. This is not an excuse—it remains each person's responsibility to manage their own resources and recognize their limitations—but it explains why the same man might show genuine empathic attunement in relaxed moments but complete empathic failure during conflict or when tired. His brain, lacking the efficient, well-practiced empathic networks that would allow perspective-taking to occur with lower metabolic cost, simply cannot allocate the resources required when other demands are high.

Women, having practiced empathic processing constantly throughout their lives, have built more efficient neural pathways that require less prefrontal effort to activate, meaning their empathy is more robust to depletion. This is not magical female nature; it is the neural consequence of thousands of hours of practice. A pianist who has practiced for years can play complex pieces while carrying on a conversation because the motor programs have become automated, requiring less conscious processing. Similarly, a woman who has spent decades practicing perspective-taking can often maintain empathic awareness even when stressed or depleted because the neural routines have become more efficient. Men who have been socially permitted to skip this practice face higher cognitive costs for empathic engagement and thus show steeper performance cliffs when under load. Understanding this dynamic allows couples to negotiate around it—recognizing that "I cannot process this right now" might be a neurobiologically accurate statement rather than an avoidance tactic—while still maintaining the expectation that men must build their empathic capacity through practice rather than simply accepting depletion as a permanent limitation.

The Neurobiology of Emotional Contagion Versus Empathy

Emotional contagion—the automatic tendency to catch others' emotions—operates through subcortical pathways involving the amygdala and can occur without conscious awareness or cognitive processing. True empathy, by contrast, requires cortical involvement, particularly in regions supporting mentalizing: the capacity to attribute mental states to others and reason about those states. Men often experience strong emotional contagion—they feel anxious when their partners are anxious, irritated when their partners are upset—but interpret these feelings as information about the situation rather than as reflections of their partners' subjective states. A man might feel tension rising during a conversation with his partner and conclude "this conversation is stressful" rather than "my partner is experiencing distress that I am detecting through emotional contagion." This misattribution means he responds to the wrong target: he tries to end the conversation to reduce his stress rather than addressing whatever is causing his partner's distress.

The dorsomedial prefrontal cortex and temporoparietal junction are critical for distinguishing self from others in emotional processing—for recognizing "this feeling I am having is actually a reflection of your feeling, not my own independent response to the situation." Women develop greater facility with this self-other distinction because their social training emphasizes understanding others' perspectives even when those perspectives conflict with their own immediate experience. Men, trained to prioritize their own perspective as objective reality, develop a less robust self-other distinction in emotional processing. When they catch their partners' emotions, they experience those emotions as their own reactions rather than as information about their partners' states. This creates the common dynamic where a woman is trying to communicate her subjective experience while a man is reporting his own emotional response to her communication, with both feeling utterly misunderstood because they are literally talking about different things without realizing it.

Neuroimaging studies of couples in conflict reveal that men show greater amygdala activation and less prefrontal regulation during disagreements, suggesting they are experiencing stronger threat responses and weaker cognitive control. Women show more balanced activation between emotional and regulatory regions, consistent with practiced skill at managing emotional arousal while maintaining cognitive processing. This difference has clear behavioral correlates: men are more likely to withdraw from conflict because their nervous systems are more easily overwhelmed. At the same time, women are more likely to pursue resolution because they have developed a greater capacity to remain engaged while emotionally activated. The withdrawal-pursuit pattern that destroys so many relationships has neurobiological roots in differential capacity for managing arousal during interpersonal stress. Men experience their withdrawal as necessary self-preservation; women experience it as abandonment. Both are neurobiologically accurate descriptions of their subjective experience, yet without understanding the underlying neural dynamics, both interpret the other's behavior through moral rather than mechanistic frameworks.

The Role of Oxytocin in Gendered Empathy

Oxytocin, often misleadingly called the "love hormone," operates very differently than popular accounts suggest and contributes to sex differences in empathic processing in complex, context-dependent ways. Oxytocin does not simply create warm feelings toward everyone; rather, it enhances attention to social cues and modulates the salience of social information. In women, oxytocin administration tends to increase attention to positive social cues and enhance empathic accuracy. In men, oxytocin administration shows more variable effects: it can improve in-group bonding while simultaneously increasing out-group suspicion and aggression. The same neurochemical amplifies social processing, but the direction of that amplification depends on contextual factors, including perceived threat, relationship security, and social learning history.

These differential oxytocin effects help explain why men often show strong empathy within narrow circles—toward romantic partners they feel securely attached to, toward their own children, toward close male friends—while showing striking empathy failures toward people outside those circles, including sometimes toward their partners during moments of perceived threat or criticism. When a man feels secure and connected, oxytocin release enhances his attention to his partner's emotional cues and increases his motivation to respond supportively. When he feels criticized or threatened, the same oxytocin system can enhance defensiveness and decrease empathic accuracy, creating the pattern where men are emotionally attuned during good times but empathically blind precisely when their partners most need them to understand. This is not intentional cruelty; it is a neurochemical system calibrated by evolution for in-group cooperation and out-group competition, now operating in intimate relationships where partners sometimes feel like allies and sometimes feel like adversaries.

Women's oxytocin systems, shaped by different evolutionary pressures and different social learning, tend to maintain empathic orientation even during conflict, though this comes at a cost: women often continue attending to and caring about their partners' emotional states even when doing so is to their own detriment. The neurochemical system that supports women's superior empathic skills also makes them vulnerable to over-empathizing, absorbing others' emotional states to the point of losing track of their own needs. Men's more contingent oxytocin responses mean they are more likely to withdraw empathy when feeling threatened, while women's more sustained empathic orientation means they are more likely to maintain empathy even when they should protect themselves. Neither pattern is optimal; both represent neural systems shaped by social contexts that may no longer serve contemporary relationship needs.

Neural Plasticity and the Possibility of Change

The most important finding from neuroscience for men seeking to improve their empathic capacity is that adult brains remain capable of substantial structural and functional change in response to sustained practice. Studies of adults who learn complex skills—from juggling to navigation to meditation—show measurable changes in both gray matter volume and white matter connectivity in relevant brain regions after weeks to months of practice. Empathy is no different: research on compassion meditation demonstrates that adults can enhance their empathic neural responses through consistent practice, showing increased activation in empathy-related brain regions and improved performance on behavioral measures of empathic accuracy. Men who deliberately practice perspective-taking, emotional awareness, and empathic responding can build more robust and more efficient empathic neural networks, effectively rehabilitating capacity that was allowed to atrophy.

This rehabilitation requires more than good intentions; it requires structured practice that challenges the brain's existing patterns. Simply trying harder to be empathic during high-stakes moments is unlikely to succeed because those moments tax the very neural resources required for empathic processing. Instead, men must practice empathic skills in low-stakes contexts where cognitive resources are available and mistakes do not carry high costs. This means deliberately practicing perspective-taking during neutral conversations, actively working to identify emotions in everyday interactions, and intentionally reflecting on others' subjective experiences during moments of calm. The goal is to build automaticity—to make empathic processing efficient enough that it remains available even under stress. This is the same principle that governs skill development in any domain: practice during low-pressure situations builds capacity that becomes accessible during high-pressure situations.

The neural evidence also reveals why defensiveness is so toxic to empathic development. When men respond to feedback about empathy failures with justification, explanation, or countercriticism, they are activating neural networks associated with threat response and self-protection rather than networks associated with learning and social connection. The dorsal anterior cingulate cortex, which activates when we detect errors or conflicts between our intentions and outcomes, must be allowed to process feedback rather than being overridden by defensive routines that shut down learning. Men who can tolerate the discomfort of recognizing empathy failures without immediately defending themselves create the neural conditions necessary for change. Those who cannot accept this discomfort—who must immediately restore their self-image as good, caring people—prevent their brains from encoding the error signal that drives learning. This means that building empathic capacity requires cultivating tolerance for shame, guilt, and self-criticism—precisely the emotions that masculine socialization teaches men to avoid through defensive posturing.

The implications are both challenging and liberating. The challenge is that improving empathic capacity requires sustained effort, consistent practice, and tolerance for the discomfort of recognizing one's own failures. There is no shortcut, no weekend workshop that will rewire decades of neural development. The liberation is that capacity genuinely exists: men are not neurobiologically doomed to empathic incompetence, and women are not biologically programmed to be empathic exhaustion sinks. Both have been shaped by social environments that pushed neural development in particular directions, and both retain the plasticity to reshape those patterns. Men who commit to building empathic capacity will initially find it effortful, cognitively demanding, and frequently unsuccessful—this is the expected trajectory of skill development, not evidence of fixed inability. With practice measured in months and years rather than days and weeks, the neural networks supporting empathy become more robust, more efficient, and more automatically activated, until what once required exhausting effort becomes natural fluency. The neuroscience reveals not that men and women are different species doomed to mutual incomprehension, but that they are individuals with varying histories of training who can, with sufficient motivation and practice, develop a shared capacity for genuine mutual understanding.

Chapter 5: Attachment Styles: How They Shape Relationships

Men frequently attribute relationship patterns to personality incompatibility, timing, or vague notions of chemistry without recognizing that beneath these surface explanations lies a more fundamental architecture: attachment style. This psychological framework, derived from decades of developmental research beginning with John Bowlby's observations of infant-caregiver bonds, reveals that the earliest relationships humans experience create internal working models of how relationships function, what intimacy means, and whether other people can be trusted to meet emotional needs. These models, formed before language and explicit memory, operate as background programming that shapes every romantic relationship an adult enters. For men, understanding attachment dynamics represents a critical opportunity to finally comprehend relationship patterns that have seemed inexplicable: why certain women seem to push them away the moment closeness develops, why others become intensely anxious when they need space, why some partners oscillate wildly between desperate clinging and hostile withdrawal. More importantly, examining their own attachment patterns allows men to recognize how their learned responses to intimacy may be systematically undermining the very connections they claim to want. The revelation that attachment is not a fixed personality but rather a learned behavioral strategy offers profound hope: what was learned in a relationship can be unlearned and relearned in a relationship, provided men are willing to engage in the uncomfortable work of examining how their earliest experiences with vulnerability, need, and trust continue to govern their adult behavior.

Attachment theory identifies four primary patterns that emerge from the intersection of two dimensions: anxiety about abandonment and avoidance of intimacy. Secure attachment, the pattern associated with healthy relationship functioning, develops when early caregivers respond consistently and appropriately to a child's needs for both comfort and autonomy. Children who experience this responsive care internalize the belief that they are worthy of love, that others are generally trustworthy, and that expressing needs leads to having those needs met rather than to rejection or overwhelm. As adults, securely attached individuals can maintain their own identity while also forming deep bonds, can tolerate conflict without catastrophizing about relationship dissolution, and can communicate directly about needs without excessive fear or defensiveness. They neither cling desperately to relationships nor maintain excessive emotional distance; they experience intimacy as nourishing rather than threatening. For men socialized into traditional masculinity, secure attachment often requires deliberate cultivation because cultural messages about self-sufficiency, emotional stoicism, and the dangers of dependence actively work against the vulnerability that secure attachment requires. Men who appear confidently independent may actually be demonstrating avoidant attachment masquerading as strength. At the same time, men who have maintained secure attachment often face accusations of being "too sensitive" or insufficiently masculine for their comfort with emotional interdependence.

Anxious attachment develops when early caregivers are inconsistent in their responsiveness, sometimes available and attuned, other times neglectful or preoccupied. Children in these environments learn that love is unreliable and must be actively secured through persistent effort and vigilance. They develop hyperactivated attachment systems that constantly scan for signs of rejection or abandonment, overinterpreting neutral behaviors as threats to connection. As adults, anxiously attached individuals crave closeness yet simultaneously fear it will be withdrawn without warning, leading to behaviors that partners experience as clingy, demanding, or emotionally volatile. They require excessive reassurance, interpret delays in text responses as catastrophic signs of waning interest, and experience their partners' need for solitude as abandonment. For women with anxious attachment, these patterns are often reinforced by cultural narratives that position women as inherently relationship-focused and men as commitment-phobic, creating a self-fulfilling prophecy where their abandonment anxiety produces controlling behaviors that push partners away, confirming their deepest fears. Men frequently misinterpret anxious attachment in female partners as "crazy" or "high-maintenance" behavior without recognizing it as a coherent strategy developed in childhood to maintain connection with unreliable caregivers. Rather than dismissing the anxiety as irrational, men who understand attachment theory recognize that for their partners, the anxiety is entirely rational given their developmental history—the problem is not that the threat detection system is malfunctioning but that it was calibrated in an environment where threats were real and is now being deployed in a context where the threats are largely historical rather than present.

Avoidant Attachment and Male Socialization

Avoidant attachment emerges when early caregivers are consistently unresponsive to emotional needs, rejecting bids for comfort or intimacy. Children in these circumstances learn that vulnerability leads to rejection, that expressing needs results in dismissal or criticism, and that safety lies in self-sufficiency rather than connection. They develop deactivated attachment systems that suppress awareness of their own needs for closeness, minimize the importance of emotional bonds, and maintain psychological distance even within ostensibly intimate relationships. As adults, avoidantly attached individuals pride themselves on independence, feel uncomfortable with expressions of need from others, and often describe partners as "too needy" when those partners are expressing normal desires for emotional connection. They excel at casual relationships but struggle when partners begin expecting deeper intimacy, often unconsciously sabotaging relationships when closeness threatens their defensive self-sufficiency. For men, avoidant attachment overlaps dangerously with cultural prescriptions for masculinity that celebrate emotional autonomy, dismiss emotional needs as weakness, and frame dependence on others as emasculating. This means that avoidantly attached men receive social reinforcement for what is actually a trauma response to early emotional neglect, making it extraordinarily difficult for them to recognize their attachment pattern as maladaptive rather than as healthy masculinity. They genuinely experience their partners' bids for emotional intimacy as excessive demands rather than as normal relationship maintenance, because their internal model of relationships does not include emotional interdependence as a legitimate component.

The collision between avoidant and anxious attachment creates one of the most common and destructive relationship dynamics, often called the anxious-avoidant trap or pursuit-distance cycle. The anxiously attached partner, detecting the avoidant partner's emotional withdrawal, becomes increasingly desperate to reestablish connection, escalating their bids for reassurance and intimacy. The avoidant partner, experiencing this increased pursuit as suffocating pressure, withdraws further to protect their autonomy, which confirms the anxious partner's fears and intensifies their pursuit. Each partner's attempt to manage their own attachment anxiety inadvertently triggers the other's, creating a self-reinforcing cycle where both people end up in maximum distress. The anxious partner feels abandoned and unloved despite being in a relationship, while the avoidant partner feels trapped and controlled despite their partner's protestations that they only want connection. Neither is consciously trying to torture the other; each is simply executing the attachment strategy they learned in childhood, unaware that those strategies are now producing exactly the outcomes they were designed to prevent. Men in this dynamic—whether as the avoidant partner frustrated by their girlfriend's "clinginess" or as the anxiously attached partner confused by their girlfriend's emotional unavailability—often lack the framework to understand that they are not dealing with personality flaws but with deeply rooted attachment patterns formed in response to early relationship environments.

Breaking this cycle requires both partners to recognize their attachment patterns and commit to acting against their instinctive responses. The anxiously attached partner must learn to self-soothe rather than constantly seeking external reassurance, tolerating the discomfort of uncertainty without immediately reaching out for confirmation of connection. This is extraordinarily difficult because it requires them to act as if the relationship is secure precisely when their nervous system is screaming that it is not. The avoidant partner must learn to lean into discomfort around vulnerability rather than reflexively withdrawing, staying present during emotional conversations even when every instinct urges them to flee or deflect. This requires them to challenge the deeply held belief that expressing needs leads to rejection, a belief that may have been entirely accurate in their childhood but is being inappropriately generalized to their current partner. For men socialized to view emotional self-sufficiency as core to their identity, this work feels like dismantling themselves, which is why so many avoidantly attached men simply exit relationships rather than do the internal work required to shift toward secure attachment. They frame their departure as "she needed too much" without recognizing that what she needed was often quite reasonable and that their inability to meet normal emotional needs reflects their own attachment limitations rather than her excessive demands.

Disorganized Attachment and Relationship Volatility

The fourth attachment pattern, disorganized or fearful-avoidant attachment, develops in childhood environments where caregivers are simultaneously the source of safety and the source of threat—typically in contexts involving abuse, severe neglect, or caregiver mental illness. Children in these situations face an impossible bind: their attachment system activates to seek comfort from the caregiver, but approaching the caregiver triggers fear because that same person is also frightening or harmful. This produces profound disorganization in which the child can develop neither a consistent strategy for seeking security nor a coherent model of how relationships work. As adults, people with disorganized attachment experience others as simultaneously desired and dangerous, leading to chaotic relationship patterns where they crave intimacy but sabotage it once achieved, push partners away but panic when they leave, or oscillate rapidly between anxious clinging and avoidant withdrawal. Their internal working models contain contradictory beliefs about self and others—"I am unlovable" coexisting with "I deserve love," "others will hurt me" alongside "I need others"—resulting in behavioral unpredictability that confuses partners who cannot discern a consistent pattern.

Women with disorganized attachment are often labeled "borderline" or "unstable" in ways that pathologize what is actually a rational adaptation to early environments where relationships were genuinely chaotic and dangerous.

Men encountering disorganized attachment in female partners often describe the relationship as a "roller coaster" where they never know which version of their partner they will encounter on any given day: the warm, loving woman who plans their future together or the hostile, withdrawn woman who insists they are fundamentally incompatible. These rapid shifts are not manipulation or game-playing; they reflect genuine oscillation between competing attachment strategies as the disorganized person's nervous system toggles between approach and avoidance without a stable default. What triggers these shifts is often invisible to partners: a perceived criticism activates the avoidant system, producing cold withdrawal; then the fear of abandonment activates the anxious system, producing desperate reconciliation attempts; then the intimacy achieved through reconciliation triggers fear of vulnerability, reactivating avoidance. Men in relationships with disorganized partners face the challenge of maintaining their own stability and boundaries while also recognizing that their partner's volatility is not fundamentally about them but about unresolved developmental trauma. This requires a sophisticated capacity to neither personalize the behavior nor dismiss its impact, to remain empathically engaged without becoming responsible for their partner's emotional regulation, and to maintain clear expectations about acceptable behavior while understanding the psychological origins of unacceptable behavior.

However, men also need to examine whether they themselves exhibit disorganized attachment patterns that they have not recognized. Male socialization often produces a specific variant of disorganized attachment where men crave the intimacy and comfort that relationships provide but have learned through repeated experiences that expressing vulnerability invites mockery, exploitation, or dismissal. These men develop approaches to relationships characterized by intense initial pursuit followed by withdrawal once real intimacy becomes possible, or by maintaining secret emotional lives because they believe their full emotional reality is unacceptable. They may describe wanting a deep connection while simultaneously structuring their lives to prevent it from developing, maintaining emotional escape routes through flirtation with other women, excessive work commitments, or substance use that numbs their awareness of intimacy needs. When partners confront this contradiction, these men often respond with genuine confusion because the internal conflict is not conscious—they truly want intimacy. Still, they are simultaneously terrified of the vulnerability it requires, leading to approach-avoidance behavior that leaves their partners exhausted and bewildered. Recognizing this pattern requires men to acknowledge that the problem is not that they have not found the right woman but that their own attachment system is generating conflicting imperatives that no partner can satisfy because the conflict is internal rather than interpersonal.

Earned Security and Relationship Repair

The most hopeful finding from attachment research is that attachment patterns, though stable, are not immutable. Adults can move toward secure attachment through sustained corrective relationship experiences that challenge their working models, a process researchers call "earned security." This typically requires prolonged exposure to a partner who responds consistently and appropriately to emotional needs, neither abandoning during conflict nor overwhelming with demands for premature vulnerability. Over time, if the anxiously attached person's bids for reassurance are met calmly rather than rejected, they begin to internalize a new model where others are reliable. If the avoidantly attached person's vulnerability is received with acceptance rather than criticism, they begin to risk deeper openness. If the disorganized person experiences sustained safety despite their testing behaviors, they begin to trust that others can be both needed and non-threatening. This neuroplastic revision of attachment models requires both partners to consciously work against their automatic responses: the secure partner must maintain patience and consistency when the insecure partner's behavior seems designed to prove that relationships inevitably fail.

In contrast, the insecure partner must tolerate the anxiety of trying new relationship strategies that contradict everything their developmental history taught them about how intimacy works.

For men seeking to develop earned security, the work often involves cultivating comfort with vulnerability states that masculinity training taught them to suppress. This might mean practicing expressing needs before those needs become crises, tolerating the discomfort of asking for comfort rather than always providing it, or staying present during emotional conversations rather than problem-solving toward quick resolution. Men with avoidant tendencies must learn that their autonomy is not actually threatened by interdependence, that having needs does not make them weak, and that their partners' emotional expressions are often information-sharing rather than demands for specific responses. Men with anxious tendencies must develop internal sources of security rather than constantly seeking external validation, learning to distinguish between genuine relationship threats and echoes of past abandonment that are being triggered by benign present circumstances. Men with disorganized attachment face the most challenging work: identifying and challenging the contradictory beliefs about relationships that generate chaotic behavior, often requiring therapeutic support to process the early trauma that created the disorganization. In all cases, the work is gradual and setback-prone, requiring men to extend themselves the same compassion they are learning to extend to others when attachment fears produce maladaptive behavior.

Women's attachment patterns also require understanding, particularly because female socialization interacts with attachment dynamics in specific ways that men often misinterpret. Women with anxious attachment may have had their natural childhood bids for connection met inconsistently, but then had those anxious tendencies amplified by cultural messages teaching them that their worth depends on securing male commitment and that men are inherently less interested in intimacy than women are. This double dose of abandonment anxiety—developmental and cultural—can produce relationship behavior that appears extreme to men who do not recognize its dual origins. Women with avoidant attachment often developed their pattern in response to childhood environments where expressing needs led to being labeled too sensitive, too emotional, or too demanding, a pattern that continues into adulthood, where female emotional needs are routinely pathologized. In contrast, male emotional withdrawal is normalized as stoic strength. Women with disorganized attachment frequently experienced childhood abuse or witnessed domestic violence, creating associations between intimacy and danger that later partners trigger unknowingly through benign behaviors that echo past trauma. Men who understand these gendered dimensions of attachment can better contextualize their partners' behaviors, recognizing that what appears to be irrational fear or excessive distance may reflect not only individual history but also cultural forces that systematically invalidate female emotional experience.

The promise of attachment theory for male-female relationships lies in its capacity to transform blame into compassion and confusion into comprehension. When a man recognizes that his girlfriend's apparent neediness reflects anxious attachment formed in a childhood where love was conditional and unpredictable, he can respond with compassion for her developmental experience rather than frustration at her current behavior. When a woman recognizes that her boyfriend's emotional withdrawal reflects avoidant attachment formed in a childhood where vulnerability led to shame, she can address his behavior as a learned defensive strategy rather than as evidence that he does not care. This reframe does not excuse harmful behavior or eliminate the need for change. Still, it repositions relationship struggles as attachment wounds seeking healing rather than as personality flaws requiring acceptance or condemnation. Men who grasp this distinction gain access to a fundamentally different relationship possibility: one where their own and their partners' most frustrating behaviors become comprehensible as protective strategies that once served crucial functions but now create the very outcomes they were designed to prevent. Armed with this understanding, men can finally move beyond reactive frustration toward the deliberate, patient work of creating the kind of consistent, responsive intimacy that allows both partners to gradually revise their attachment models toward greater security, building relationships characterized not by the absence of attachment injuries but by the mutual commitment to healing them together.

Chapter 6: Cultural Conditioning: Unpacking Gender Roles

The architecture of gender expectations operates like an invisible operating system installed before conscious awareness, running background programs that shape behavior, perception, and possibility throughout human lives. Unlike biological sex or even gender identity—concepts that have received extensive cultural attention—gender roles represent the behavioral scripts, social expectations, and performance mandates that culture assigns based on perceived gender. These roles are not natural expressions of innate difference but rather elaborate social constructions maintained through reward and punishment systems so pervasive that they become indistinguishable from reality itself. For men attempting to understand women, the most critical realization is that women are not mysterious creatures operating according to incomprehensible logic; they are humans performing within a radically different set of cultural constraints that shape everything from career aspirations to emotional expression to spatial movement through the world. Men, meanwhile, perform their own culturally assigned roles with equal lack of awareness, mistaking socially constructed masculinity for authentic selfhood and interpreting their own conditioning as evidence of natural male essence. The result is two groups of humans whose behavior has been systematically shaped by asymmetrical social forces, each believing their own performance represents genuine nature. In contrast, the other represents confusing deviance from normalcy.

Cultural conditioning begins not at birth but before it, as parents-to-be imagine futures constrained by the perceived sex of their fetus. Research in developmental psychology demonstrates that parents describe fetal movement differently depending on whether they believe they are carrying a boy or a girl: identical levels of activity are characterized as "vigorous" and "strong" for presumed males, "gentle" and "delicate" for presumed females. This interpretive divergence continues through infancy, where studies using gender-neutral babies dressed in stereotype-congruent or incongruent clothing reveal that adults handle, speak to, and play with the same infant differently based solely on clothing cues suggesting gender. Babies perceived as male are bounced more vigorously, encouraged toward physical exploration, and offered toys emphasizing action and problem-solving. Babies perceived as female are held more carefully, spoken to with a higher pitch and more elaborate vocabulary, and provided toys emphasizing nurturance and appearance. By eighteen months—long before children can articulate gender concepts—these differential treatment patterns have produced measurable differences in behavior, spatial skills, and social responsiveness that adults then cite as evidence of innate sex differences, completing a self-fulfilling prophecy that erases the months of systematic shaping that produced the outcomes.

The preschool years intensify gender role enforcement through peer policing that operates with remarkable brutality. Children who violate gender norms—boys who prefer quiet play or express emotions beyond anger, girls who reject appearance-based activities or demonstrate physical aggression—face swift social correction from both peers and adults. Boys learn that the worst possible insult is comparison to girls or femininity, establishing a hierarchy where masculinity is defined negatively as the absence of anything feminine rather than positively as a coherent identity. Girls learn that their value correlates with physical attractiveness and social accommodation, receiving praise for being "sweet," "helpful," and "pretty" while receiving correction for being "bossy," "loud," or "wild." Educational research tracking teacher interactions reveals that boys receive more attention overall, more encouragement to solve problems independently, and more feedback focused on the quality of their work. In contrast, girls receive more feedback focused on compliance, neatness, and following directions. Teachers call on boys more frequently, even when girls raise their hands more often, ask boys more complex questions requiring analytical thinking, and grant boys more latitude for physical movement and noise while enforcing stricter behavioral standards for girls. These patterns, replicated across thousands of interactions over years, construct fundamentally different learning environments that shape not just what children know but how they come to understand themselves as learners and thinkers.

The Spatial Politics of Gender Performance

Gender roles extend beyond behavior and emotion into the physical realm of space occupation and bodily autonomy, creating vastly different experiences of moving through the world. Men are socialized to occupy space expansively—sitting with legs spread, walking with a confident stride, taking up room in public spaces without apologizing or minimizing their physical presence. This spatial entitlement becomes so naturalized that men experience it as simple comfort rather than recognizing it as learned behavior that communicates dominance and claims territory. Women, conversely, are trained from girlhood to make themselves smaller: crossing legs, tucking elbows, apologizing when others bump into them, moving aside to let others pass even when they have the right of way. Urban planning research analyzing pedestrian behavior on sidewalks reveals that women alter their paths to avoid collisions far more frequently than men, who maintain their trajectories, expecting others to accommodate them. This is not a biological difference in spatial awareness but learned patterns of entitlement versus accommodation that render women responsible for preventing collisions. At the same time, men move through public space as though they possess inherent priority.

The female body itself becomes a site of cultural regulation in ways men rarely experience or recognize. Women learn that their bodies are simultaneously public property subject to commentary and evaluation, and dangerous objects that must be carefully managed to avoid "provoking" male attention or violence. The advice women receive—don't walk alone at night, watch your drink, dress modestly, don't lead men on—positions female bodies as perpetually responsible for male behavior, requiring constant vigilance and self-limitation. Dress codes in schools and workplaces disproportionately target girls and women, framing female bodies as inherently distracting to men whose attention and productivity must be protected through female concealment. These policies teach girls that their education is less important than boys' comfort, that their bodies are problems requiring management, and that male desire is simultaneously female responsibility and female fault. Boys internalize these same messages, learning that female bodies exist primarily for their consumption and evaluation, that their sexual responses override female autonomy, and that women who fail to properly regulate their appearance have forfeited the right to boundaries. When men later express bewilderment at women's "paranoia" about safety or irritation with women's "obsession" with appearance, they are revealing their ignorance of the surveillance systems women navigate daily, where bodies are simultaneously objectified and blamed, desired and punished.

The performance of femininity requires extensive invisible labor that men neither perform nor recognize as work. Anthropological studies examining time-use patterns reveal that women spend significantly more time and money on appearance maintenance than men, not because they are naturally more vain but because social and professional penalties for failing to meet feminine presentation standards are severe. Women who do not perform sufficient femininity through makeup, styled hair, carefully curated clothing, and body modification are perceived as less competent, less promotable, and less socially acceptable. Research in organizational behavior demonstrates that women who present as too feminine are dismissed as lightweight and incompetent. In contrast, women who present as insufficiently feminine are penalized as cold and unlikable, creating a narrow acceptability window that requires constant calibration. Men face no equivalent double bind; they can achieve professional credibility and social acceptance through a basic standard of grooming that requires minimal time and thought. When men complain about the time women spend "getting ready" or dismiss feminist critiques of beauty standards as trivial, they are demonstrating their inability to perceive that what looks like personal choice is actually compliance with mandatory performance standards enforced through real professional and social consequences.

Occupational Segregation and the Devaluation of Women's Work

Gender roles extend into occupational domains through mechanisms so subtle that they maintain segregation and wage disparities while appearing neutral or merit-based. Labor economists have documented that occupations become devalued as they feminize—the same work commands lower wages and prestige when performed primarily by women than when performed primarily by men. Computer programming began as female-dominated work considered clerical and detail-oriented, then transformed into male-dominated technical work with significantly higher compensation once men entered the field and reframed the same tasks as requiring logic and innovation. Elementary education, once a male profession commanded by schoolmasters, lost prestige and relative compensation as it became female-dominated and was reconceptualized as nurturing work rather than intellectual leadership. This pattern repeats across occupations: as women enter a field, the work is culturally reconceptualized as requiring stereotypically feminine traits, those traits are devalued as less skilled despite requiring sophisticated capabilities, and compensation decreases accordingly. Men benefit from this system through occupational advantage even in female-dominated fields, where they experience glass escalators that preferentially promote them to leadership positions. At the same time, women face glass ceilings that prevent advancement.

The devaluation extends beyond pay into the fundamental conceptualization of what counts as work. Activities associated with women—particularly care work, domestic labor, and emotional support—are framed as natural expressions of female nature rather than skilled labor deserving compensation. This ideological move, which historian Nancy Fraser terms "social reproduction," renders essential work invisible while positioning it as women's natural duty rather than as labor that sustains the paid economy. Men can succeed in professional domains only because someone performs the uncompensated work of maintaining households, raising children, managing social relationships, and providing emotional support—work disproportionately performed by women. The heterosexual family structure historically solved capitalism's need for this unpaid labor by positioning wives as economically dependent on husbands whose wages theoretically covered both partners' contributions. As women entered paid employment without men proportionally increasing their domestic contributions, women now perform double shifts of paid and unpaid work. In contrast, men continue to benefit from the social reproduction of labor that enables their careers. Men who claim they support gender equality while expecting female partners to manage household operations, coordinate family schedules, and provide emotional support without equivalent reciprocity are performing what sociologists call "egalitarian espousal with traditional enactment"—verbally endorsing equality while behaviorally maintaining traditional privilege.

Professional environments enforce gender role compliance through subtle penalties that maintain segregation even within ostensibly integrated fields. Women in male-dominated professions face constant credibility challenges requiring repeated demonstrations of competence that men do not face, experience exclusion from informal networks where key information and opportunities circulate, and encounter hostile environments where their presence is framed as diversity hiring rather than merit-based achievement. Management research examining performance evaluations reveals that women receive significantly more feedback focused on communication style and personality traits— described as "abrasive," "aggressive," or "difficult"—while men receive feedback that concentrates on technical skills and strategic thinking. Women who negotiate for raises or promotions are penalized as unlikable and pushy, while identical behavior in men is rewarded as leadership and confidence. These patterns persist even when researchers control for actual performance, revealing that evaluation systems do not objectively measure competence but rather measure conformity to gendered expectations about how workers should behave. Men in female-dominated professions face inverse dynamics but ultimately benefit from them: male nurses and elementary teachers are channeled toward specializations and leadership positions considered more appropriate for their gender, experiencing faster advancement than female colleagues.

Relationship Scripts and the Performance of Heterosexuality

Heterosexual relationship dynamics operate according to deeply gendered scripts that position men as initiators, pursuers, and decision-makers while positioning women as gatekeepers who regulate access while appearing passive. Dating rituals in contemporary Western cultures still largely follow courtship patterns where men are expected to ask women out, plan dates, initiate physical intimacy, and eventually propose marriage—all while women are expected to make themselves attractive and available but not too eager, to express interest but not too directly, to participate but not to lead. These scripts create asymmetrical vulnerabilities: men face rejection when initiating, women face physical and social dangers when accepting. The stakes differ not just in degree but in kind: male ego versus female safety, male embarrassment versus female violence. Yet cultural narratives frame male vulnerability in romantic pursuit as the primary relationship risk while minimizing or completely erasing the calculations women must constantly perform about whether accepting a date, entering a private space, or declining unwanted attention will result in harm.

These relationship scripts extend into marriage through the gendered division of domestic responsibilities that persists even in dual-income households where both partners work full-time. Time-use studies across industrialized nations consistently demonstrate that women perform significantly more housework and childcare than male partners, with the gap narrowing slightly but remaining substantial even among couples who explicitly espouse egalitarian values. The persistence of this inequality despite changing gender ideology suggests that cultural conditioning operates at levels deeper than conscious belief, manifesting in automatic assumptions about whose responsibility it is to notice when laundry needs doing, whose career accommodates childcare disruptions, and whose standards determine household cleanliness. Men in heterosexual partnerships often describe "helping" with housework or "babysitting" their own children, linguistic constructions that reveal their conceptualization of domestic labor as fundamentally female responsibility that they occasionally assist with, rather than a shared obligation they co-own. Women, meanwhile, perform what sociologists term the "mental load" or "cognitive labor" of household management—tracking what needs doing, planning sequences, remembering deadlines, and delegating tasks—even when men perform the physical execution, meaning women never experience true cognitive offloading even when the visible labor appears shared.

Sexual scripts within heterosexual relationships encode particularly rigid gender roles that position male pleasure as the primary goal and female pleasure as secondary or decorative. Sexuality research examining orgasm gaps in heterosexual versus same-sex encounters reveals striking disparities: heterosexual women report significantly fewer orgasms than men in hookup contexts, with the gap narrowing but not disappearing in relationship contexts. In contrast, lesbian women report orgasm rates comparable to heterosexual men. This disparity is not biological—women's bodies are perfectly capable of reliable orgasm as demonstrated by same-sex data—but cultural, reflecting socialized patterns where male orgasm is understood as the natural conclusion of sex. In contrast, female orgasm is a bonus when it occurs, but not the definition of whether sex "counts" as having happened. Young women receive socialization that frames their role in sex as pleasuring male partners while managing their own boundaries against male pressure, learning that their desires are less legitimate than male desires and that prioritizing their pleasure makes them selfish or demanding. Young men receive complementary socialization that frames sex as something they obtain from women who restrict access, positioning female desire as gatekeeping rather than as equivalent sexual subjectivity deserving accommodation.

Jordan Ashford

The Trap of "Natural" Differences

Perhaps the most powerful mechanism maintaining gender role rigidity is the constant appeal to biological essentialism that reframes culturally constructed patterns as natural inevitabilities. When confronted with evidence of gender disparities in any domain—wages, leadership representation, domestic labor, spatial behavior, emotional expression—defenders of the status quo immediately invoke evolutionary psychology, hormones, or brain differences to explain why current arrangements reflect natural order rather than social construction. These appeals serve a powerful ideological function: they position inequality as an unfortunate biological reality rather than as an injustice requiring remedy, absolving those who benefit from challenging their advantage or examining their complicity. The irony is that many of the "natural" differences invoked to justify gender arrangements emerge only under conditions of gender-differentiated socialization; when researchers study infants too young to have absorbed cultural gender norms or examine cultures with different gender configurations, many supposedly universal sex differences disappear or reverse.

The scientific literature on sex differences reveals far more within-group variation than between-group differences for virtually every psychological and cognitive trait measured. The distributions for men and women overlap substantially, with most individuals falling in ranges indistinguishable between sexes. Yet cultural narratives cherry-pick the small measurable differences while ignoring the massive overlaps, constructing a story of profound male-female difference that the data do not support. Neuroscientist Gina Rippon's research on brain imaging studies demonstrates that many widely cited findings about male and female brains either fail to replicate or represent tiny effect sizes that have been sensationalized in popular media. More fundamentally, the brain's neuroplasticity means that any differences observed in adult brains cannot be straightforwardly attributed to biology versus experience; decades of gender-differentiated treatment produce neurological changes that are then cited as evidence of innate difference, completing circular reasoning that mistakes outcome for cause. When men cite "science" to justify their disinterest in emotional labor or their expectation that female partners will accommodate their careers, they are not neutrally describing biology but rather deploying a selective interpretation of contested research to rationalize maintaining privilege.

The concept of natural gender differences also conveniently ignores the enormous cross-cultural and historical variation in gender role assignments. Anthropological research documents societies where behaviors considered essentially masculine or feminine in Western contexts are understood as gender-neutral or assigned to the opposite gender. Margaret Mead's classic studies of New Guinea cultures found societies where women were expected to be assertive and men gentle, societies where both genders performed similar roles, and societies with gender configurations entirely different from Western patterns. Historical research reveals that Victorian-era medical authorities believed women were too delicate for higher education and would damage their reproductive systems through intellectual effort—a "biological fact" that conveniently disappeared when economic conditions required educated female workers. Contemporary debates about whether women can perform in combat positions, handle high-stress leadership roles, or maintain objectivity in scientific research recycle identical rhetoric once used to exclude women from voting, owning property, and obtaining credit, suggesting these arguments serve ideological rather than empirical functions. Each generation's gender restrictions claim foundation in immutable biology, then quietly adjust when social conditions change, revealing that what passes for natural law is actually cultural preference dressed in scientific language.

The damage of biological essentialism extends beyond its use in justifying inequality to its constriction of human possibility for both women and men. When culture declares certain traits, interests, or capabilities naturally masculine or feminine, it channels humans into narrower ranges of development than their actual capacities would support. Men who might excel at early childhood education, nursing, or social work encounter cultural messages that these fields are feminized and therefore unsuitable, depriving both them and society of their talents. Women who might thrive in mechanical trades, computer science, or executive leadership face identical channeling away from their aptitudes through cultural messaging about natural female preferences. The cost is not just to individuals who are diverted from paths where they could flourish but to entire societies that fail to benefit from fully utilizing human capital. When men defend gender role arrangements by citing nature, they are not protecting inevitable biological reality but rather protecting cultural systems that limit both sexes while disproportionately benefiting men through unearned advantages that feel like natural entitlement.

Understanding cultural conditioning requires men to confront an uncomfortable reality: much of what they experience as their authentic self is actually the internalization of masculine role requirements that began shaping them before conscious memory. The emotional restriction, the competitive orientation, the discomfort with vulnerability, the assumption of spatial entitlement, the expectation that others will perform support labor—these are not natural male traits but learned performances that have been so thoroughly normalized they feel like inherent identity. Recognizing this constructedness does not mean male identity is false or that men must abandon everything masculine; rather, it means distinguishing between freely chosen expressions of self and compulsory performances of cultural masculinity. The work of unpacking gender conditioning allows men to selectively retain aspects that genuinely serve them while discarding aspects that harm both them and their relationships. It permits men to recognize that women's apparently incomprehensible behavior often represents rational responses to different cultural constraints, and that improving relationships requires not just understanding women better but examining how men's own conditioning creates barriers to the intimacy they claim to want. Most fundamentally, it requires accepting that discomfort with this examination is itself a product of masculine conditioning that frames self-reflection as weakness—and that pushing through that discomfort is necessary for growth that no shortcut can provide.

Chapter 7: The Reality of Boundaries: Respect and Recognition

The concept of boundaries has been thoroughly domesticated in popular psychology, reduced to therapeutic platitudes about "setting limits" and "learning to say no" that strip away the profound political and relational implications of boundary dynamics. Men frequently encounter boundary language as a set of arbitrary rules women impose—mysterious lines that appear without warning, shift without logic, and function primarily as obstacles to male desire. This framing misses the fundamental reality: boundaries are not capricious restrictions but rather the architectural blueprints of selfhood, the demarcations that define where one person ends and another begins. For women, boundary assertion represents an act of existential self-definition in a cultural context that has historically denied them the right to occupy space, refuse demands, or prioritize their own needs over others' comfort. When men fail to recognize, respect, or even perceive women's boundaries, they are not merely being inconsiderate—they are participating in a larger pattern of erasure that treats female autonomy as negotiable rather than foundational. The challenge for men is not learning a new set of social rules but rather developing the capacity to recognize that women possess independent subjectivity that does not exist in service of male needs, desires, or convenience.

The difficulty begins with the fundamental asymmetry in how boundaries are socialized. Boys learn boundaries primarily as territorial concepts—physical spaces, possessions, and zones of control that others must not violate. A boy's room is his castle, his toys are his property, and intrusions require his permission. This creates an internal model where boundaries are external perimeters defending the self against incursion. Girls, conversely, are socialized to have porous boundaries that prioritize others' access over their own autonomy. A girl who refuses to hug relatives is corrected for being rude; a girl who declines to share is called selfish; a girl who expresses discomfort with physical affection is told she is being difficult or hurting others' feelings. The message is unmistakable: female boundaries are subordinate to others' emotional needs, particularly when those others are male. By adolescence, this conditioning produces young women who struggle to articulate boundaries because doing so requires claiming a right to autonomous selfhood that has been systematically denied throughout their development. They may know something feels wrong, but lack the internalized permission to name their discomfort as valid grounds for refusal. This is not weakness or confusion—it is the predictable result of fifteen years of training that their primary function is accommodating others rather than defining and defending their own limits.

The professional domain reveals how thoroughly boundary violations have been normalized as the price of female participation in public life. Women in male-dominated workplaces navigate a constant barrage of boundary intrusions that operate below the threshold of formal complaint but above the threshold of comfort: colleagues who stand too close during conversations, who touch lower backs or shoulders without invitation, who comment on physical appearance in ways that reduce professional identity to decorative function. Men often defend these behaviors as friendliness or compliments, genuinely baffled when women express discomfort. What men miss is the cumulative weight of dozens of small violations that communicate a consistent message: your bodily autonomy is secondary to my impulse to touch, comment, or access. Each incident may seem trivial, but the pattern constitutes chronic boundary erosion that forces women to choose between tolerating violations or being labeled oversensitive, humorless, or unable to handle workplace culture. Research in organizational behavior examining women's attrition from high-status professions reveals that "culture fit" problems frequently translate to exhaustion from constant boundary defense in environments where male comfort with boundary-crossing behavior is treated as the neutral baseline that women must accommodate rather than challenge.

The Consent Continuum and Boundary Negotiation

Sexual consent has finally entered mainstream discourse, yet most conversations remain trapped in a binary framework—yes or no, consent or assault—that obscures the vast middle territory where most boundary negotiations actually occur. This binary thinking serves men poorly because it suggests that anything short of explicit refusal constitutes permission, a standard that ignores the reality of coerced consent, freeze responses, and the sophisticated compliance mechanisms women develop to manage male reactions to refusal. Women describe experiences of saying yes when they meant no because saying no felt dangerous, of participating in sexual activity they did not want because the emotional or physical cost of declining seemed higher than the cost of compliance, of performing enthusiasm to manage male ego when they felt nothing but the desire for the encounter to end. These experiences do not fit neatly into legal categories of assault. Yet, they represent profound boundary violations that leave lasting impacts on women's relationship to their own sexuality and their trust in male partners' capacity to prioritize female autonomy over male gratification.

The prevalence of these gray-zone experiences reveals that consent is not a single moment of agreement but rather an ongoing negotiation that requires continuous attention to a partner's engagement, enthusiasm, and comfort. Men socialized to view sex as a prize to be won or a goal to be achieved often approach consent mechanically—obtaining initial agreement and then proceeding as though that agreement constitutes blanket permission for everything that follows. This fundamentally misunderstands consent as a relational process rather than a transactional exchange. A woman who agrees to kissing has not consented to touching; a woman who agrees to touching has not consented to sex; a woman who agrees to sex has not consented to particular acts, intensities, or durations. Each escalation requires fresh attunement to whether she remains engaged and enthusiastic rather than compliant and enduring. Men frequently protest that this standard feels impossibly demanding, requiring constant checking-in that disrupts spontaneity and passion. This complaint reveals the problem: these men have eroticized female passivity and framed active female participation as a barrier to their pleasure rather than as the foundation of ethical sexuality. Truly consensual sex—where both partners remain actively engaged in negotiating what happens next rather than one partner pushing forward while the other manages their response—does not require awkward interruptions because continuous attunement becomes integrated into the sexual dynamic itself.

The concept of enthusiastic consent attempts to address these gray zones by establishing that meaningful consent requires active desire rather than mere absence of refusal. This standard unsettles many men because it eliminates the ambiguity that has historically worked in their favor. If consent requires enthusiasm, then men can no longer interpret silence, passivity, or ambivalence as permission. They must develop the capacity to read their partners' genuine engagement and the willingness to stop when that engagement falters, even if stopping means not getting what they wanted. This represents a profound shift in who bears the burden of boundary negotiation: rather than women being responsible for clearly articulating "no" in contexts where doing so may be socially, emotionally, or physically risky, men become responsible for ensuring "yes" is genuine, ongoing, and enthusiastic. Men often experience this standard as unfair, arguing that women should simply be direct about what they want and do not want. This argument ignores the entire context in which female sexual refusal occurs—contexts where women have learned through direct experience that male responses to "no" range from sulking and guilt-tripping to aggression and violence, making compliance safer than refusal in many situations.

Physical Space and the Entitled Male Body

The male body moves through physical space with an assumption of entitlement that renders itself invisible through sheer ubiquity. Men do not notice they are taking up extra space on public transit, interrupting women's paths on sidewalks, or standing too close during conversations because these behaviors feel natural rather than chosen. Transportation researchers analyzing subway and bus seating patterns using time-lapse photography have documented that men occupy an average of 1.3 seats worth of space through spread legs, splayed arms on armrests, and bags placed on adjacent seats, while women average 0.7 seats through compressed posture and belongings held in laps. When women request that men close their legs to free up space, they are frequently met with indignation or claims of biological necessity—that male anatomy requires leg spreading for comfort. This explanation fails basic anatomical scrutiny: the degree of spread that men perform vastly exceeds any biomechanical requirement, and the fact that this behavior intensifies in crowded spaces suggests territorial display rather than physical necessity. The real discomfort men experience when asked to contain their bodies is not anatomical but psychological— it requires relinquishing the spatial privilege they have naturalized as neutral existence.

The dynamics of physical proximity reveal how thoroughly men have been granted permission to penetrate women's personal space without invitation or consequence. Stand-up comedy routines observe that women spend significant time avoiding strange men who stand too close in lines, elevators, or parking lots. In contrast, men rarely notice these spatial calculations because they are not the targets of such intrusions. Proxemics research examining comfortable interpersonal distances finds that people generally maintain larger buffer zones around men than around women. Still, men violate women's personal space boundaries significantly more frequently than the reverse, particularly in workplace and service-industry contexts where women's professional roles require tolerating proximity they would refuse in social settings. A male manager who places his hand on a female employee's shoulder while reviewing her work, who leans over her to point at her computer screen, or who stands close enough during conversation that she can feel his breath is crossing intimate distance thresholds that would be unacceptable between male colleagues. Yet these violations are so routine that identifying them as problematic makes women appear hypersensitive rather than the man appearing boundary-incompetent.

The politics of touch underscore how male physical access to female bodies has been socially constructed as a male right rather than a female-granted privilege. Women describe constant unwanted touching from men in professional and social contexts: handshakes that transform into lingering hand-holds, goodbye hugs from casual acquaintances, hands on lower backs guiding them through doorways, shoulder squeezes meant as encouragement, hair-touching accompanied by compliments. Each touch individually may seem innocuous, but the aggregate effect is profound: women's bodies are treated as semi-public property available for male tactile consumption regardless of whether permission has been granted. Men defend these touches as affectionate, friendly, or meaningless, often expressing hurt feelings when women establish no-touch boundaries. This response is revealing—it positions male comfort with touching as more important than female comfort with being touched, framing women's bodily autonomy as an offense against male affectionate expression. The entitlement goes deeper than individual men's behavior; it is woven into social scripts that make it extraordinarily difficult for women to refuse touch without seeming cold, rude, or inappropriately formal. A woman who steps back when a male colleague approaches for a hug, who keeps her hand brief during handshakes, or who verbally declines physical contact faces social penalties for violating the expectation that she will absorb male tactile attention gracefully.

Emotional Boundaries and the Male Right to Female Processing

Emotional boundaries represent perhaps the most invisible form of boundary violation in male-female dynamics because the intrusion does not appear as transgression but rather as a male need that women should naturally want to meet. Men who would never consider themselves boundary violators often construct relationships where their female partners function as unpaid therapists, emotional processors, and mood regulators, performing sophisticated psychological labor that goes unrecognized as such. The man who arrives home stressed and immediately begins venting to his partner, the man who processes every workplace conflict through extensive conversation with his girlfriend, the man who requires his wife's emotional support through every personal challenge—these men are treating female emotional capacity as an infinitely available resource rather than recognizing it as finite energy that their partners might need for their own psychological work. Women are socially trained to provide this support without keeping track of reciprocity, without marking it as labor, and without establishing limits on how much of their emotional bandwidth can be claimed by others' needs.

The pattern becomes particularly corrosive when men use female partners as emotional dumping grounds while simultaneously dismissing those partners' emotional needs as excessive or dramatic. Men describe feeling relaxed and unburdened after venting to their partners, but describe feeling drained and overwhelmed when their partners seek similar processing support. This asymmetry reveals that these men have internalized a model where their emotional experiences warrant serious attention while their partners' emotional experiences represent burdens to be minimized. Sociological research on heterosexual couples' communication patterns finds that men interrupt women significantly more than women interrupt men. Still, more importantly, men's topics of conversation receive more sustained attention and elaboration while women's topics are more frequently redirected, abbreviated, or dismissed. This creates relationships where one person's internal world becomes the shared focus while the other person's internal world remains peripheralized—a profound boundary violation that goes unrecognized because it aligns with larger cultural patterns positioning male subjectivity as central and female subjectivity as supporting infrastructure.

The expectation that women will manage not just their own emotions but also male emotions represents a particularly insidious boundary violation because it co-opts women's emotional capacity in the service of male emotional regulation. When a man becomes angry and his partner must carefully modulate her responses to avoid escalating his anger, she is performing emotional labor that treats his feelings as her responsibility. When a man withdraws into sulking silence and his partner must draw him out, interpret his mood, and address his unstated grievances, she is doing cognitive and emotional work that should be his responsibility. When a man makes a mistake and his partner must reassure him, minimize the error, and rebuild his confidence rather than simply processing her own response to the mistake, she is prioritizing his emotional state over her legitimate reactions. These patterns are not mutual caregiving—they are unidirectional emotional service that positions women as responsible for maintaining male psychological equilibrium. At the same time, men bear no equivalent responsibility for female emotional states.

The Boundary Violation of Explanation Demands

Women exist in a perpetual state of being required to explain, justify, and defend their boundaries to men who position themselves as entitled to detailed accounts of female decision-making. When a woman declines a date, she is expected to provide a reason; when she ends a relationship, she must offer a comprehensive explanation; when she expresses discomfort with a situation, she needs to articulate precisely why the situation troubles her in ways men find legitimate. This demand for explanation functions as a boundary violation in itself because it treats female autonomy as requiring male approval—a woman's "no" is not sufficient on its own but must be accompanied by justification that men deem reasonable. Men rarely notice they are doing this because the demand feels like a reasonable request for information rather than an assertion that women's choices belong to male jurisdiction. A man who responds to romantic rejection by asking "but why?" or "what did I do wrong?" or "is there someone else?" is not seeking information—he is implicitly communicating that her preference alone is insufficient grounds for refusal and that he deserves an explanation that will help him either accept the rejection or construct an appeal.

The explanation demand extends beyond romantic contexts into every domain where women make choices that inconvenience or disappoint men. A woman who declines to stay late at work must explain her evening plans; a woman who does not smile at a stranger's greeting must account for her rudeness; a woman who leaves a social gathering early needs to justify her departure beyond simply not wanting to be there anymore. Men grant themselves the right to leave jobs, relationships, conversations, and social situations whenever they choose without detailed justification. Still, women who exercise equivalent autonomy are positioned as owing explanations that satisfy male assessment of whether their reasons meet some standard of legitimacy. This double standard operates because male agency is culturally presumed, while female agency requires justification—men are assumed to have good reasons for their choices. In contrast, women's choices are suspect until proven otherwise. The exhaustion women experience in this dynamic comes not from making choices but from the requirement that every choice be defended against implicit challenge.

The deeper violation is that the explanation demands that men function as opportunities for men to negotiate boundaries rather than respect them. When a man asks why a woman does not want to go on a second date, he is often seeking information that will allow him to address her concerns and change her mind rather than accepting her decision as final. When a man asks why his partner needs space, he is positioning her boundary as negotiable rather than absolute. This transforms every boundary assertion into a debate where women must not only articulate their limits but also defend them against counterarguments, evidence that their concerns are overblown, or appeals to give the man another chance. Women learn through these experiences that boundaries are never fully secure—that even after saying no, they must continue defending the refusal against ongoing attempts to erode it. The result is that women often avoid setting boundaries at all, choosing instead to tolerate violations rather than engage in the exhausting work of defending boundaries against men who treat female autonomy as a position to be argued against rather than a fact to be acknowledged.

Recognizing Boundaries Before They Are Articulated

The most sophisticated form of boundary respect involves perceiving limits before they must be explicitly stated, recognizing discomfort before it escalates to verbal refusal. This requires the development of what might be called boundary literacy—the ability to read subtle signals of hesitation, disengagement, or discomfort and respond by pausing, checking in, or withdrawing pressure rather than proceeding until a clear "no" forces cessation. Men often claim this is an impossible standard, arguing that they cannot read minds and that women need to communicate clearly. This argument positions boundary literacy as telepathy rather than recognizing it as attentiveness to observable behavioral data. A woman who stops reciprocating in physical contact, whose body goes still, who provides increasingly brief verbal responses, who avoids eye contact, or whose facial expressions shift from engagement to neutrality or distress is communicating clearly through nonverbal channels that men have learned not to read because they prefer the plausible deniability that comes from attending only to words.

Research in nonverbal communication demonstrates that humans are extraordinarily skilled at detecting subtle emotional states in others when motivated to do so—detecting deception, reading dominance hierarchies, and interpreting romantic interest all rely on processing micro-expressions, postural shifts, and tonal variations. Men apply these skills constantly in professional and social contexts where reading others accurately serves their interests. The claim that they cannot detect female discomfort is not about capability but about priority: men have learned that attending carefully to female comfort often means stopping behaviors they want to continue, so they have developed motivated blindness that allows them to proceed while claiming ignorance. A man who would immediately notice and respond to a male friend's discomfort during a conversation somehow becomes unable to detect equivalent or more pronounced signals from a woman during a sexual encounter. This is not a neurological deficit—it is willful inattention protected by cultural narratives that position male pleasure as important enough to warrant risk. At the same time, female discomfort is not important enough to warrant caution.

Developing genuine boundary literacy requires men to shift from a permission-seeking framework to an attunement framework. Permission-seeking asks, "Has she said no?" and proceeds until that threshold is reached. Attunement asks, "Is she actively engaged, comfortable, and enthusiastic?" and pauses when those indicators are absent. This shift seems subtle but represents a fundamental reorientation of responsibility: instead of women being responsible for clearly articulating boundaries that stop male forward momentum, men become responsible for continuously monitoring whether their forward momentum is genuinely welcomed. This requires accepting uncertainty—proceeding only when signals are clearly positive rather than proceeding whenever signals are not clearly negative. For many men, this feels like an unfair burden because it means sometimes stopping when continuation might have been acceptable. But this is precisely how boundary respect works in contexts men already understand: a surgeon does not continue operating whenever a patient has not explicitly withdrawn consent; they monitor vital signs continuously and stop at any indication of distress. The fact that men can understand this principle in medical contexts but resist applying it to sexual and relational contexts reveals that the resistance is not about comprehension difficulty but about the desire to prioritize male satisfaction over female safety.

The transformation required is not learning new information but rather valuing female autonomy highly enough that protecting it becomes more important than maximizing male sexual or emotional access. Men who genuinely prioritize their partners' boundaries develop sophisticated attunement almost automatically because they are motivated to notice and respond to discomfort rather than motivated to avoid noticing discomfort that would require them to stop. This motivation shift cannot be taught through lists of warning signs or behavioral guidelines—it emerges from the deeper work of recognizing women as fully autonomous subjects whose internal experiences matter as much as men's, whose comfort is as important as male pleasure, and whose boundaries deserve respect not because respecting them serves male interests but because boundaries are the architecture of human dignity that must never be subordinated to another person's convenience.

Chapter 8: Decoding Emotional Strength: Vulnerability as Power

The contemporary discourse around masculinity has produced a curious paradox: men are simultaneously told they need to "open up" emotionally while receiving virtually no instruction on what emotional openness actually entails or why it matters beyond appeasing female partners. The result is performative vulnerability—men who have learned to recite the language of feelings without developing genuine emotional literacy, who mistake confession for connection, and who treat vulnerability as a tactical concession rather than recognizing it as the foundation of psychological resilience. Women, meanwhile, have spent generations navigating a different paradox: their emotional expressiveness is simultaneously demanded as proof of femininity and dismissed as evidence of weakness, their capacity for vulnerability positioned as both their greatest asset in relationships and their fundamental liability in professional and public life. Understanding vulnerability as power requires dismantling these distorted frameworks entirely and recognizing that what gets labeled "emotional strength" in men—stoicism, self-sufficiency, emotional containment—often represents not strength at all but rather a brittle defensiveness that fractures under pressure. In contrast, what gets dismissed as female "over-emotionality" frequently represents sophisticated emotional processing that men have never learned to value because they have never needed to develop it.

The misunderstanding begins with the conflation of vulnerability with weakness, a conceptual error that pervades masculine socialization and distorts men's relationship to their own emotional lives. Vulnerability, properly understood, is not the state of being wounded or helpless but rather the willingness to experience and acknowledge emotional states without immediately defending against them, transforming them, or forcing them into more comfortable configurations. It is the capacity to sit with uncertainty, to admit when one does not know, to recognize emotional needs without shame, and to allow others to witness one's interior experience without editing that experience to manage their reactions. This is extraordinarily difficult psychological work that requires what psychologists call "distress tolerance"—the ability to experience uncomfortable emotional states without immediately acting to eliminate the discomfort. Women develop high distress tolerance through necessity; they spend their lives experiencing emotions that social convention prohibits them from fully expressing or that others dismiss as invalid, forcing them to metabolize feelings internally while maintaining external composure. Men, granted social permission to externalize discomfort through anger or to simply exit situations that produce uncomfortable feelings, often develop remarkably low distress tolerance despite cultural narratives that frame male stoicism as emotional fortitude. When a man says he "doesn't do feelings," he is often describing not strength but avoidance—an inability to remain present with emotional experience that he has learned to frame as masculine self-control rather than recognizing it as a developmental gap.

The Physiological Architecture of Emotional Suppression

Recent advances in psychophysiology have revealed that emotional suppression carries measurable biological costs that accumulate over time, producing health consequences that disproportionately affect men precisely because masculine socialization encourages chronic suppression as a default operating procedure. When individuals suppress emotional expression—whether by inhibiting facial expressions, controlling vocal tone, or dampening physiological arousal—their bodies exhibit increased sympathetic nervous system activation, elevated blood pressure, and heightened production of stress hormones including cortisol and catecholamines. This creates a physiological state similar to chronic low-grade threat response, where the body remains in subtle but persistent activation even when no external danger exists. Epidemiological research tracking cardiovascular outcomes has documented that men who report high levels of emotional restrictiveness show significantly elevated rates of hypertension, coronary disease, and sudden cardiac events compared to men who report greater emotional expressiveness, even after controlling for other risk factors, including smoking, diet, and exercise. The mechanism appears to involve both the direct physiological cost of suppression and the indirect effects of chronically elevated stress hormones on vascular health, immune function, and inflammatory processes.

Women who engage in emotional suppression—particularly in professional contexts where emotional expression is penalized—show similar physiological costs, suggesting the issue is not gendered biology but rather the act of suppression itself. However, women generally have access to emotional expression outlets that men lack: female friendships that normalize emotional disclosure, cultural permission to seek therapy or support, and reduced social penalties for acknowledging psychological struggle. Men, socialized to view emotional disclosure as feminine and therefore degrading, often lack any regular venue for emotional expression, meaning their suppression is not situational but chronic. The cumulative physiological burden manifests not only in cardiovascular outcomes but in the documented male vulnerability to stress-related illness, higher rates of completed suicide despite lower rates of depression diagnosis, and the well-established mortality gap wherein men die younger than women across virtually all developed nations. What gets framed as male biological fragility may be better understood as the accumulated cost of emotional suppression demanded by masculine ideals that position vulnerability as antithetical to male identity. The tragic irony is that the defensive armor men construct to protect themselves from perceived emotional weakness becomes the mechanism of their actual physical destruction.

Vulnerability as Information Processing Advantage

Beyond the health consequences of suppression, emotional vulnerability serves critical cognitive functions that rational-minded men consistently undervalue because they have been taught to conceptualize thinking and feeling as opposing processes rather than recognizing emotion as a sophisticated information system that provides data unavailable through purely analytical reasoning. Emotions represent rapid-response evaluation systems that integrate vast amounts of contextual information and generate action-relevant assessments faster than conscious deliberation can operate. When someone experiences a "gut feeling" about a person or situation, they are accessing pattern-matching processes that have aggregated countless micro-observations—vocal prosody, facial microexpressions, postural cues, contextual incongruities—into an intuitive judgment that conscious analysis might take hours to reconstruct. Neuroscience research using patients with damage to emotion-processing regions demonstrates that these individuals, despite intact logical reasoning, make catastrophically poor decisions because they lack the emotional guidance systems that normally prioritize options and signal which outcomes matter. They can analyze decision trees rationally but cannot determine which branches to pursue because they have lost access to the feeling-based value assignments that make certain futures desirable and others aversive.

Women's greater comfort with emotional awareness provides them with systematic advantages in domains requiring interpersonal assessment, risk evaluation, and complex decision-making under uncertainty—all contexts where purely analytical approaches fail because relevant variables exceed computational capacity or because the most critical information exists in relational dynamics rather than objective facts. When a woman says she has "a bad feeling" about someone her male partner trusts, she is often detecting genuine signals of untrustworthiness that his more limited emotional attunement has not registered. When she advocates against a decision that "looks good on paper" because something "feels off," she may be integrating contextual subtleties that formal analysis has excluded. Men's frequent dismissal of these emotion-based assessments as irrational or paranoid represents a profound failure to recognize that emotional information is still information—indeed, often more accurate and comprehensive than the limited data sets that rational analysis can consciously process. The man who prides himself on making "logical decisions" while ignoring emotional input is not being more objective; he is simply making decisions based on incomplete information, having excluded an entire category of relevant data because his socialization has taught him to devalue anything bearing the taint of feeling.

The business world has slowly begun recognizing what it terms "emotional intelligence" as critical to leadership effectiveness, yet this recognition remains superficial because it treats emotional capabilities as supplementary soft skills rather than fundamental cognitive tools. Effective executives must read organizational dynamics, assess stakeholder motivations, navigate political complexities, and inspire collective action—all tasks that depend heavily on emotional attunement and relational intelligence. Studies examining leadership failures in corporate contexts reveal that technical competence combined with emotional obtuseness produces leaders who alienate teams, miss early warning signs of organizational dysfunction, and make strategically sound decisions that fail in execution because they ignore human factors. The most successful leaders, regardless of gender, demonstrate sophisticated emotional processing: they perceive morale problems before they show in metrics, they detect resistance beneath apparent compliance, they sense when someone needs support versus challenge, and they modulate their own emotional expression strategically to influence group dynamics. These are not innate charisma but learnable skills that require practice in emotional awareness—precisely the practice that masculine socialization discourages in men while demanding it in women, who must develop emotional sophistication as a survival strategy.

The Relational Mechanics of Trust Construction

Vulnerability operates as the primary mechanism through which human beings establish trust and construct intimate relationships. Yet, men are systematically underprepared to engage this process because masculine ideals position self-disclosure as a strategic weakness rather than a relational necessity. Research in relationship development demonstrates that trust does not emerge from reliability or competence alone but rather through graduated mutual disclosure wherein each party reveals progressively more sensitive information, observes how the other handles that information, and uses those observations to calibrate how much additional trust to extend. This process requires both parties to take risks—sharing information that could be used against them, exposing needs that might be dismissed, revealing uncertainty or inadequacy that could diminish their status—and then experience those risks being honored rather than exploited. Each successful cycle of disclosure-and-honoring deepens the relationship; each failure to honor disclosure damages trust, sometimes irreparably.

Men enter this process at a severe disadvantage because they have spent their lives avoiding exactly the kind of disclosure that trust construction requires. They have learned to present curated versions of themselves that emphasize strength, competence, and self-sufficiency while concealing doubt, need, and struggle. They have developed sophisticated defensive strategies—humor that deflects genuine emotional content, intellectual analysis that transforms feelings into abstract problems, anger that replaces more vulnerable emotions like hurt or fear—that prevent them from engaging in authentic disclosure even when they consciously want a deeper connection. Women repeatedly describe the frustration of male partners who claim to want intimacy but refuse the vulnerability that intimacy requires, who complain about feeling disconnected, but who will not disclose the internal experiences that would allow connection to form. These men are not deliberately withholding; they are caught in a double bind where their longing for intimacy conflicts with their deeply ingrained prohibition against the vulnerability through which intimacy is built. They want the destination without traveling the required path, want to be known without being willing to be seen, want connection without surrendering the defensive armor that prevents connection from forming.

Women's greater facility with vulnerability gives them a significant advantage in relationship formation and maintenance. Still, this advantage comes at a cost: women's willingness to be vulnerable makes them systematically more exposed to exploitation, dismissal, and betrayal from male partners who have not developed reciprocal vulnerability capacity. When women disclose struggles, they risk having those struggles weaponized in later arguments or used to justify dismissing their perspectives. When they express needs, they risk being labeled needy or high-maintenance. When they share fears or insecurities, they risk having their partners lose respect for them or become contemptuous. The asymmetry is brutal: women must practice vulnerability to establish intimacy, but their vulnerability is often met not with reciprocal disclosure but with masculine discomfort, advice-giving, or subtle contempt for weakness that men would never tolerate in themselves. Men benefit from this arrangement by receiving the intimacy that women's vulnerability creates without having to engage the vulnerability themselves, positioning themselves as the strong partners supporting weak women rather than recognizing that their female partners are demonstrating advanced relational capabilities that they lack.

Vulnerability Hangover and Defensive Reactivity

One particularly destructive pattern that men must recognize in themselves is what relationship researchers term "vulnerability hangover"—the experience of retrospective shame or anxiety following emotional disclosure that leads individuals to defensively retract, minimize, or attack their own previous openness. Men who have been socialized to view emotional expression as weakness often experience profound discomfort after moments of genuine disclosure, even when their partners respond supportively. This discomfort manifests as secondary defensive reactions: minimizing what they shared ("I was just tired, I didn't mean all that"), intellectualizing it ("I was just thinking about stress response patterns"), getting angry at their partners for "making" them be vulnerable, or creating emotional distance to reestablish the protective barrier they temporarily lowered. Women who witness this pattern describe feeling whipsawed—their partners open up meaningfully, they respond with care and support, and then their partners punish them for having seen the vulnerability, often through withdrawal, irritability, or criticism that seems to come from nowhere.

The vulnerability hangover reveals that the obstacle to male emotional openness is not merely a lack of skill or practice but active discomfort with the self that emotional disclosure reveals. Men who have constructed their identities around strength, competence, and self-sufficiency experience genuine identity threat when they acknowledge need, uncertainty, or weakness—even in the private context of intimate relationships. Therapy research tracking male clients reveals that men frequently report feeling worse rather than better after sessions involving emotional disclosure, describing the experience as "losing it" or "falling apart" rather than recognizing it as healthy emotional processing. This negative subjective experience makes subsequent disclosure less likely, creating a reinforcement schedule where vulnerability is punished by internal shame even when external responses are supportive. Breaking this pattern requires men to develop what psychologists call "meta-cognitive awareness"—the ability to observe their own reactions without being controlled by them—so they can notice the vulnerability hangover occurring and consciously choose not to act on the defensive impulses it generates.

Women attempting to support male partners through vulnerability hangover face impossible terrain: responding with too much care and attention can feel infantilizing to men who are already destabilized by having shown weakness, while not responding enough leaves them feeling exposed and unsupported. Women describe walking this tightrope constantly, trying to honor their partners' disclosure without making a "big deal" out of it, affirming without gushing, being present without being intrusive. The emotional labor required is immense, and the margin for error is razor-thin. Men who want genuine intimacy must take responsibility for managing their own vulnerability hangovers rather than expecting their partners to navigate the defensive aftermath of their emotional disclosure. This means developing self-awareness about when the hangover is occurring, communicating about it rather than acting out from it, and consciously resisting the impulse to create distance or pick fights as a way to reestablish emotional equilibrium. It means recognizing that the discomfort following vulnerability is not evidence that vulnerability was a mistake but rather evidence that one is challenging deeply ingrained defensive patterns—and that growth occurs precisely in that discomfort.

The transformation from viewing vulnerability as weakness to recognizing it as strength requires men to fundamentally redefine what strength means. True strength is not the absence of difficult emotions or the ability to suppress them; it is the capacity to experience emotions fully without being overwhelmed by them, to acknowledge needs without shame, to remain present with discomfort rather than reflexively defending against it. This definition of strength is far more demanding than masculine stoicism because it requires ongoing engagement with internal experience rather than simply numbing or externalizing it. Women have known this all along—their emotional expressiveness is not evidence of weakness but rather a demonstration of the psychological resilience required to feel deeply while remaining functional. Men who dismiss this as "over-emotionality" are not demonstrating superior strength; they are revealing their own underdeveloped capacity to tolerate emotional experience. The path forward requires men to approach vulnerability not as a concession to female preferences but as essential work of developing their own psychological capabilities, work that has been deferred too long at enormous cost to their health, their relationships, and their fundamental human capacity to be known and to know themselves.

Chapter 9: The Impact of Male Fragility: Women's Adaptation Strategies

The phenomenon of male fragility—the defensive, often disproportionate reaction men display when their competence, authority, or worldview is challenged—operates as one of the most consequential yet least examined forces shaping heterosexual relationships. Unlike the familiar concept of "toxic masculinity," which focuses on overtly aggressive or domineering behavior, male fragility manifests as a brittleness at the core of masculine identity that makes even minor feedback or disagreement feel like existential threats. This fragility creates a gravitational field around which women must constantly orbit, adjusting their communication, calibrating their achievements, and managing their own needs to avoid triggering defensive reactions that range from sulking withdrawal to explosive anger. The exhausting irony is that men who consider themselves rational, thick-skinned, and emotionally resilient often exhibit the most pronounced fragility when confronted with information that threatens their self-concept. A man who prides himself on being logical may respond with barely concealed hostility when his partner gently corrects a factual error. A man who claims to value equality may spiral into defensive justifications when asked to contribute more equitably to household labor. A man who insists he wants honest communication may punish that honesty with days of cold distance when his partner expresses disappointment in his behavior. These reactions are not character flaws of individual men but rather predictable consequences of socialization that teaches males their value rests on never appearing wrong, weak, or uncertain—a standard that renders genuine learning and growth nearly impossible because both require admitting current limitations.

Women develop elaborate adaptation strategies to navigate male fragility, strategies so sophisticated and automatic that both parties often fail to recognize them as adaptations at all. These strategies function as a parallel operating system running constantly in the background, scanning for fragility triggers and preemptively adjusting behavior to minimize defensive reactions while still attempting to achieve basic relationship goals. The most fundamental adaptation is what might be called "ego cushioning"—the practice of wrapping necessary information in layers of reassurance, praise, and strategic framing designed to allow men to receive correction or criticism without experiencing it as an attack on their fundamental competence. A woman who needs her partner to load the dishwasher differently does not simply demonstrate the more effective method; she prefaces the information with acknowledgment of his effort, frames the correction as a peculiarity of their particular dishwasher rather than a deficit in his understanding, and often adds self-deprecating comments about her own learning curve with the appliance. This elaborate packaging is not passive-aggressive indirectness but rather a calculated strategy developed through experience: direct correction, even when delivered neutrally, triggers defensiveness that transforms a ten-second interaction about dish placement into a twenty-minute conflict about respect, nagging, and whether she appreciates anything he does.

The cognitive load required for constant ego cushioning is staggering yet remains largely invisible to the men who benefit from it. Women describe the mental process as running multiple simultaneous calculations: What information needs to be conveyed? How will he likely interpret this, given his current state and recent history? What framing will allow him to hear it without becoming defensive? What reassurances need to be preloaded? What tone will communicate both clarity and non-threat? How can I position this as collaborative problem-solving rather than criticism? This complex calculus happens in real-time, often multiple times per conversation, transforming what should be a straightforward information exchange into elaborate diplomatic negotiations. Men, meanwhile, experience themselves as simply participating in normal discussions, entirely unaware that nearly every piece of potentially challenging information has been carefully pre-processed by their partners to protect them from the discomfort of direct feedback. When women, exhausted by this constant labor, finally deliver information without cushioning, men experience it as a sudden, inexplicable shift in communication style—she used to be so understanding and now she is harsh and critical—without recognizing that her "understanding" style was actually intensive emotional labor performed specifically to manage his fragility.

Strategic Incompetence Recognition and Counter-Adaptation

One of the most corrosive expressions of male fragility manifests as strategic incompetence around domestic and emotional labor, where men perform tasks so poorly that women eventually assume responsibility to avoid the consequences of continued male "failure." What makes this dynamic particularly complex is that male fragility transforms attempts to address strategic incompetence into attacks on masculine competence, creating a double bind where women cannot point out the pattern without triggering the very defensiveness that maintains it. Women have developed counter-adaptations that attempt to circumvent this trap, strategies that range from gamification to calculated withdrawal, each with its own costs and limitations. Some women adopt what organizational psychologists call "deliberate delegation with scaffolding"—breaking tasks into components simple enough that failure becomes implausible while providing just enough structure that men can succeed without requiring constant oversight. This transforms women into managers of their own households, creating detailed systems, reminder protocols, and step-by-step instructions that theoretically enable male competence but actually represent additional unpaid labor while doing nothing to develop genuine male capacity for initiative or complex task management.

Other women deploy strategic withdrawal, consciously allowing systems to fail rather than continuing to compensate for male incompetence. This approach, while theoretically sound as a boundary-setting mechanism, collides directly with male fragility in ways that often make it unsustainable. When birthday parties go unplanned because a man failed to calendar them, when children arrive at school without the required materials. A man did not read the weekly update email. When social relationships atrophy because a man never initiates contact, the consequences typically fall most heavily on women and children. In contrast, men experience only abstract awareness that something was supposed to happen. More significantly, when women stop compensating, male fragility often manifests as wounded bewilderment—"Why didn't you remind me?" or "I didn't know this was important to you"—that reframes female withdrawal of unpaid labor as female failure to communicate properly rather than as male failure to develop basic life management skills. This rhetorical move exploits the male fragility's defense mechanism. By positioning himself as willing but insufficiently informed, a man avoids confronting his own incompetence while maintaining the moral high ground as someone who would have done the right thing if only she had explained it clearly enough.

A third adaptation strategy involves what sociologists studying domestic labor call "preemptive over-functioning," where women simply absorb all complex tasks rather than engaging in the exhausting process of teaching, monitoring, and managing male participation. This adaptation acknowledges the reality that delegation itself represents work, often work exceeding the effort required to simply do the task oneself, and that male fragility makes delegation emotionally costly in ways that must be factored into any efficiency calculation. A woman who can plan a birthday party in an hour but would need three hours to delegate it to her partner (including the emotional labor of managing his defensiveness about needing instruction and his resentment at being "assigned tasks like a child") makes a rational economic choice by absorbing the work herself. The tragedy is that this adaptation, while locally optimal, globally reinforces male incompetence while eroding women's wellbeing through unsustainable workload and mounting resentment. Women in this pattern often describe feeling profoundly alone in their relationships despite cohabitation with partners—they are running entire households and families as solo operations while simultaneously managing a dependent adult whose primary contribution is not creating additional problems.

Professional Achievement Modulation

Male fragility extends beyond domestic contexts into professional and intellectual domains, where women learn to modulate their achievements, ambitions, and competence to avoid threatening male partners whose identities depend on being the more successful member of the couple. This adaptation manifests differently across educational and economic levels but follows a consistent pattern: women make themselves smaller professionally to preserve relationship stability, carefully calibrating how much success they can display before it triggers partner insecurity. Research examining dual-career couples finds that women employ numerous strategies to minimize the visibility and significance of their professional accomplishments: downplaying promotions or salary increases, attributing success to luck or circumstance rather than skill, redirecting conversations about their achievements to their partners' work, and sometimes declining opportunities that would create too great a disparity in status or income. These behaviors are not symptoms of a female's lack of ambition but rather sophisticated social intelligence recognizing that male partners often respond to female professional success with subtle or overt punishment that makes the achievement pyrrhic.

The punishment for female success takes forms that maintain plausible deniability while effectively constraining women's professional growth. A man whose partner earns more than he does may not explicitly demand that she refuse her promotion. Still, he may increase his criticism of her parenting, become less available for childcare, withdraw emotionally, or develop mysterious health or psychological issues requiring increased support precisely when her career demands intensify. These responses, whether conscious or unconscious, function to impose costs on female achievement that discourage future advancement. Women facing such dynamics must choose between career growth and relationship stability, a choice their male partners never confront because female partners typically respond to male success with increased support rather than increased criticism. The fragility underlying these dynamics reveals itself when women attempt to discuss the pattern directly:

men become defensive about accusations of insecurity, frame their partner's professional focus as neglect of the relationship, or present themselves as supportive. At the same time, their behavior consistently undermines her capacity to succeed.

Some women adapt by pursuing what economists call "sequential rather than simultaneous optimization"—they suppress their own career ambitions during the partnership-building and child-rearing years, planning to pursue professional goals once the relationship is secure and children are older. This strategy, while rational given the constraints, systematically disadvantages women because career capital accumulates most rapidly during precisely the years when women are strategically underinvesting in professional development to manage male fragility and perform disproportionate domestic labor. Women who attempt to relaunch careers after years of accommodation discover they are competing with workers who spent those same years building skills, networks, and credentials, while also often facing partners who have become accustomed to being the primary status-holder and resist the identity adjustment required when their partner develops independent professional standing. The adaptation that seemed to preserve relationship harmony while postponing conflict actually forecloses options and concentrates vulnerability, leaving women economically dependent on partners whose fragility they must continue managing indefinitely.

Conversational Labor and Topic Management

Women perform constant conversational labor to navigate male fragility around intellectual authority, managing not just what information is shared but how it is delivered, in what contexts, and with what level of certainty. This adaptation begins with topic selection—women learn which subjects their partners consider themselves authoritative on and avoid contradicting that authority directly, even when they possess superior knowledge or insight. When a woman knows more about a topic than her male partner, she faces a choice between sharing her expertise and risking his defensive reaction or remaining silent and allowing his incomplete or incorrect understanding to stand. Neither option is satisfying:

sharing knowledge triggers fragility-based pushback that transforms information exchange into ego defense, while remaining silent means accepting that relationship harmony depends on protecting male authority even at the cost of accuracy and female intellectual contribution. Women describe developing elaborate internal calculi for deciding which battles are worth fighting—generally limiting corrections to situations where the stakes are high enough to justify the emotional labor and defensive reaction that will follow.

When women do offer information that challenges male understanding, they deploy sophisticated face-saving strategies designed to allow men to integrate new information without experiencing it as a correction. These strategies include attributing the information to a third party rather than claiming it as personal knowledge ("I read somewhere that..."), framing it as recently discovered rather than long-held understanding ("I just learned that..."), presenting it as a question rather than a statement ("I wonder if it might be..."), or positioning themselves as confused and seeking clarification ("Maybe I'm misunderstanding, but..."). Each of these framings allows men to incorporate the information while maintaining the psychological stance of teacher or authority figure rather than student or error-maker. The sophistication required to execute these strategies while participating in actual substantive conversation is extraordinary—women must simultaneously engage with content, monitor their partner's emotional state, select appropriate framing strategies, and modulate tone and body language to communicate both competence and deference. Men experiencing these conversations typically notice only the content level, remaining entirely unaware of the paralinguistic labor their partners are performing to allow information to flow without triggering defensiveness.

The cumulative effect of this conversational labor is that women become intellectually smaller in their relationships, contributing less than their full knowledge and insight to avoid managing male fragility. Over time, this adaptation can lead to intellectual atrophy—when women habitually censor their contributions, they begin to doubt their own knowledge and capacity, internalizing the message that their understanding is less valid than their partners' even in domains where they possess superior expertise. This internalization serves male fragility perfectly: women who have been trained to question their own competence pose less threat to male authority and require less active suppression. The relationship appears harmonious because women have so thoroughly adapted that they no longer consciously register all the moments they choose silence over contribution, all the insights they withhold, all the corrections they swallow. Men in these relationships often describe their partners as less intellectually engaged than they were early in the relationship, attributing the change to female disinterest rather than recognizing it as the predictable outcome of systematic punishment for female intellectual contribution.

Emotional Processing Delegation and Its Consequences

Perhaps the most damaging adaptation women develop in response to male fragility involves what clinical psychologists call "emotional outsourcing"—women become responsible not only for processing their own emotional experiences but also for processing their male partners' emotions because men cannot tolerate the vulnerability required for emotional self-examination. This extends far beyond the emotional labor of maintaining relationships; it requires women to serve as auxiliary nervous systems for men who experience emotions but lack either the skills or the willingness to examine those emotions without defensive deflection. When a man feels inadequate but cannot acknowledge his inadequacy, his partner must somehow address the underlying insecurity while allowing him to maintain conscious belief in his competence. When a man feels angry about something but cannot examine what actually triggered the anger, his partner must reconstruct the emotional logic. At the same time, he denies having complex feelings at all. When a man feels afraid or uncertain but cannot tolerate acknowledging fear, his partner must validate and soothe without naming what she is validating and soothing because naming it would constitute exactly the acknowledgment he cannot bear.

This adaptation requires women to develop extraordinary psychological sophistication—they must understand their partners' emotional landscapes better than their partners understand those landscapes themselves, while also pretending not to understand because explicit acknowledgment of male emotion triggers male fragility. Women describe this dynamic as emotionally claustrophobic: they are responsible for their partners' emotional well-being but prohibited from directly addressing emotional content because doing so requires their partners to acknowledge having emotions that need addressing. The result is elaborate choreographies of indirect emotional management where women must engineer situations that allow men to feel better without ever explicitly discussing what they were feeling or why. A woman whose partner is struggling with professional insecurity might strategically arrange activities that allow him to demonstrate competence, initiate conversations where others affirm his capabilities, and avoid any situations that might highlight his limitations—all while pretending this elaborate management is simply how she naturally organizes their shared life rather than intensive therapeutic intervention.

The cost of this adaptation extends beyond the immediate labor to long-term relationship viability. Women who serve as emotional processors for fragile male partners accumulate resentment at the asymmetry—they must handle not only their own emotional complexity but also their partners' complexity while receiving no reciprocal support because their partners' fragility precludes them from engaging with difficult female emotions. More insidiously, this dynamic positions women as responsible for male emotional regulation in ways that replicate mother-child patterns rather than adult partnerships. Women find themselves analyzing their partners' moods, strategizing about how to improve those moods, feeling responsible when their partners are unhappy, and developing the same combination of fierce protectiveness and frustrated resentment that characterizes parental relationships with emotionally immature children. This transformation from partner to emotional parent fundamentally alters relationship dynamics, often destroying sexual attraction and breeding contempt that women struggle to acknowledge because it conflicts with their investment in viewing their relationships as equitable partnerships between adults.

The adaptation strategies women develop around male fragility collectively constitute a shadow curriculum of female socialization—lessons girls and women learn through direct experience about the necessity of managing male ego while pursuing their own goals within carefully policed boundaries. These strategies, while demonstrating remarkable ingenuity and sophisticated social intelligence, exact enormous costs in cognitive load, emotional exhaustion, career limitation, intellectual suppression, and relationship authenticity. Understanding these adaptations is essential for men genuinely committed to building equitable partnerships because it reveals how thoroughly women have accommodated to male limitations. In contrast, those limitations remain invisible to the men who carry them. The work of dismantling male fragility begins with recognition: acknowledging that what feels like normal interaction to men often represents intensive female labor performed to protect men from confronting their own brittleness, and committing to developing the emotional resilience required to receive feedback, acknowledge limitation, and tolerate the discomfort of not being right without making that discomfort women's problem to solve.

Chapter 10: The Invisible Load: The Unseen Work Women Do

The domestic sphere operates according to physics most men never learn: objects do not return themselves to their proper locations, food does not spontaneously appear in refrigerators organized by expiration date, appointments do not manifest on calendars through sheer necessity, and social obligations do not fulfill themselves through collective wishful thinking. Behind the seeming effortlessness of functional households lies an intricate architecture of cognitive labor that women perform so seamlessly that its absence, not its presence, finally renders it visible. This invisible load encompasses far more than the physical tasks tracked by time-use studies, which already document women's disproportionate contribution to domestic work. The deeper inequity lies in the mental labor of household management: the planning, anticipating, researching, deciding, remembering, and monitoring that transforms a house into a functioning home and a collection of individuals into a coordinated family unit. Men frequently believe they contribute equally to household labor because they complete assigned tasks, failing to account for the metacognitive work of determining what tasks exist, when they must be completed, what resources they require, and who should complete them. This task-identification and task-assignment labor remains so thoroughly invisible that men experience their partners as inexplicably anxious or controlling rather than recognizing them as systems administrators managing complex operations that would immediately collapse without their constant oversight.

The invisibility of this load stems partly from its preventative nature—successful household management means problems never materialize, rather than problems being solved after they arise. A woman who notices the family is nearly out of laundry detergent and adds it to the shopping list before the last load creates an entirely different outcome than waiting until the shortage produces a crisis. Yet her foresight generates no visible product; from her partner's perspective, detergent simply exists when needed, its presence unremarkable and apparently automatic. The same preventative logic applies across thousands of household domains: scheduling doctor's appointments before health issues become acute, purchasing birthday gifts weeks in advance rather than scrambling last-minute, noticing when children have outgrown clothing before they have nothing appropriate to wear, maintaining relationships with extended family before they atrophy into estrangement, rotating pantry stock to prevent spoilage, monitoring household supplies to avoid running out of necessities. Each of these acts represents multiple cognitive steps—noticing current state, projecting future need, identifying solutions, evaluating options, executing decisions, and monitoring outcomes—yet produces no tangible evidence of work performed. Men inhabit homes where the future has been carefully managed into smooth continuity with the present, never experiencing the friction of system failure that would reveal the labor preventing it.

The Project Management of Daily Life

Contemporary households function as complex projects requiring coordination across multiple domains, timelines, and stakeholders. Yet, most families operate without formally designated project managers, defaulting instead to gendered assumptions that women will naturally assume this role. The cognitive demands of household project management rival those of professional roles: maintaining comprehensive awareness of the status of dozens of simultaneous initiatives, tracking dependencies where task B cannot begin until task A completes, managing resource constraints of time and money, communicating expectations to various participants who possess different skill levels and reliability profiles, and adjusting plans dynamically as circumstances change. A typical week might require coordinating: grocery shopping that accounts for upcoming schedule disruptions, meal planning that accommodates dietary restrictions and preferences while minimizing waste, appointment scheduling that optimizes travel time across multiple family members, coordination with schools regarding permission slips and volunteer commitments, monitoring and responding to various digital communication channels, planning social engagements, managing household maintenance issues, tracking medication and health needs, and ensuring adequate supplies of mundane necessities from toilet paper to printer ink.

The mental load of maintaining situational awareness across these domains means women carry a working memory constantly populated with incomplete tasks, upcoming deadlines, and contingency plans. This cognitive burden manifests neurologically: studies using experience sampling methods that prompt participants at random intervals throughout the day to report what they are thinking reveal that women report thinking about household and family management tasks significantly more frequently than men, even when both partners are engaged in the same activity. A couple watching television together inhabits entirely different cognitive environments—he is watching the show, she is watching the show while simultaneously tracking that their daughter needs new shoes before next week's field trip, that the car registration expires soon, that her mother mentioned feeling isolated during their last call, that the pediatrician appointment needs rescheduling, and that they are hosting dinner Saturday requiring grocery shopping by Friday. This split attention is not a deficit or a distraction but rather the ordinary cognitive state of household managers who cannot fully disengage from their management responsibilities even during leisure. The exhaustion women report is partly sleep deprivation and physical labor, but more fundamentally, it reflects the metabolic cost of maintaining extensive active working memory with no designated off-hours. Men, unburdened by this background processing, possess cognitive resources for hobbies, focused attention on single tasks, and genuine relaxation—privileges they experience as simply normal human capacity rather than recognizing them as enabled by someone else's labor.

The Research Burden and Decision Fatigue

Every household decision that appears simple from the outside conceals extensive research labor that typically falls to women. Selecting a pediatrician requires not merely choosing from available options but first researching what factors should inform the decision, investigating individual providers' credentials and approach to care, reading reviews from other parents, verifying insurance coverage, assessing office location and hours against family logistics, and synthesizing all this information into a defensible recommendation. This pattern repeats endlessly: choosing summer camps, evaluating schools, selecting insurance plans, researching large purchases, investigating symptoms before medical appointments, identifying appropriate birthday gifts for extended family, finding reliable service providers for household repairs, and comparing vacation options. Each research project demands hours of cognitive work—formulating evaluation criteria, gathering information from multiple sources, assessing credibility and relevance, weighing trade-offs, and documenting findings. The labor intensifies when household members hold strong preferences or when decisions carry significant consequences, adding emotional pressure to the cognitive burden of research.

The cumulative effect of constant decision-making produces what psychologists term "decision fatigue"—the deterioration of decision quality after making many decisions in sequence, as the mental resources required for evaluating options become depleted. Research in behavioral economics demonstrates that decision fatigue leads to decision avoidance, impulsive choices, or defaulting to status quo options rather than engaging in the effortful analysis required for optimal decisions. Women managing households make dozens of decisions daily—what to prepare for meals, what to pack in school lunches, what activities to prioritize when time is limited, how to respond to behavioral issues, whether to address conflicts with teachers or coaches, how to allocate limited budgets across competing needs—each demanding cognitive resources that are never fully replenished because the decision-making never stops. Men experience decision fatigue primarily in professional contexts where they make consequential choices, then return home to environments where major decisions have already been researched and framed as simple preferences: "Do you want chicken or fish for dinner?" obscures the thirty minutes of meal planning, recipe research, inventory checking, and nutritional consideration that preceded the question. When men do participate in household decisions, they often approach them as isolated events requiring fresh research rather than as nodes in ongoing informational networks that women have been maintaining continuously. A man asked to choose a birthday gift for his mother may spend an hour researching options that his partner could have identified in minutes by drawing on her continuously updated knowledge of his mother's interests, recent purchases, and expressed needs—knowledge that did not accumulate accidentally but through deliberate attention and relationship maintenance labor.

The Default Parent Phenomenon

In households with children, the invisible load intensifies dramatically through the phenomenon of the "default parent"—the parent who holds ultimate responsibility for children's wellbeing regardless of which parent is physically present or nominally in charge. The default parent maintains comprehensive awareness of children's schedules, developmental needs, social dynamics, academic progress, health status, emotional states, and emerging challenges. This parent knows without checking which child needs a science project completed by Thursday, which is struggling with a particular friendship, which has a mild peanut allergy requiring communication with party hosts, which is due for a dentist appointment, and which has outgrown winter clothes requiring replacement before cold weather arrives. The non-default parent—typically the father—may be actively involved in childcare, spending substantial time with children and performing discrete parenting tasks, yet operates within a system maintained by the default parent's comprehensive awareness. He can successfully take children to the park because the default parent ensured they had appropriate clothing, sunscreen, snacks, and scheduled the outing to avoid conflicting with nap times or other obligations. His ability to function as a competent parent during his parenting time depends entirely on the infrastructure the default parent maintains.

The default parent asymmetry reveals itself most clearly when that parent is unavailable. When mothers travel for work, they typically prepare detailed instructions covering routines, schedules, food preferences, location of supplies, contact information for schools and activity coordinators, and contingency plans for likely issues.

Fathers traveling for work typically walk out the door, assuming their partners will seamlessly maintain all household and childcare operations without documentation because they are simply doing what they always do. This is not because fathers are callous but because they genuinely do not perceive the extent of management labor their partners perform continuously. Mothers preparing for absence must essentially create externalized versions of their working memory—explicit documentation of knowledge that normally exists as tacit awareness—because they recognize their partners do not carry this information as part of their ordinary cognitive load. The emotional burden of default parenthood extends beyond practical coordination into existential responsibility: the default parent experiences children's struggles as their struggles to solve, children's unhappiness as their failure to provide, and children's unmet needs as their inadequacy. Non-default parents can feel concern and sympathy while maintaining psychological distance that frames these issues as problems the family faces rather than problems they personally must resolve.

Social Reproduction and Relationship Maintenance Across Networks

The invisible load extends beyond household boundaries into the social infrastructure that connects families to extended networks of relatives, friends, schools, and communities. Women perform what sociologists call "kinship work"—the labor of maintaining family relationships across generations and geographical distance through cards, calls, gift-giving, visit coordination, and conflict mediation. This work ensures that children know their grandparents, that siblings remain connected despite diverging life paths, that aging parents receive attention and support, and that family traditions persist across generations. Men benefit from these maintained relationships without recognizing that relationships require maintenance. A man enjoys close connections with his siblings partly because his partner has been coordinating group gatherings, facilitating communication during conflicts, remembering to send congratulations for achievements, and ensuring his parents receive attention on significant occasions. Research on social network maintenance documents that women initiate contact with both their own and their partners' extended family members at significantly higher rates than men, send more greeting cards and gifts, make more effort to attend family events, and invest more energy in relationship repair after conflicts. When these relationships flourish, men often attribute success to natural family closeness rather than recognizing the deliberate cultivation their partners provide.

The labor extends similarly to friendship networks, school communities, and neighborhood relationships. Women coordinate social plans for couples, maintain connections with friends from various life stages, ensure children's friendships are supported through playdates and birthday parties, volunteer at schools to remain informed about educational environments, advocate for their children, and build neighborhood networks that provide mutual support and information exchange. Each of these relationship domains requires ongoing attention: remembering details of others' lives to inquire about meaningfully, initiating contact with appropriate frequency, reciprocating invitations and assistance, navigating conflicts or hurt feelings, and calibrating relationship investment across multiple connections with varying intimacy levels and maintenance requirements. Men often describe their social lives as mysteriously diminishing after marriage, not recognizing that bachelor social networks were likely smaller and more activity-based rather than relationship-based. In contrast, married social life involves more complex relationship webs that require more sophisticated maintenance—maintenance that their partners provide. When couples divorce, men frequently experience dramatic social isolation, not because people choose sides, but because their ex-partners had been maintaining the relationship infrastructure that connected them to the community. Friends stop calling not from loyalty to the ex-wife but because the ex-wife had been the one scheduling gatherings, sending updates, and doing the emotional labor that sustained the friendships through which the husband accessed social connection.

The Anticipatory Time Horizon

One of the most cognitively demanding aspects of the invisible load is maintaining extended time horizons, anticipating needs and obligations weeks or months in advance, and ensuring present actions position the household appropriately for future requirements. Women describe constantly "thinking ahead"—a phrase that sounds simple but represents sophisticated temporal planning across multiple calendars and contingency scenarios. A mother in June is already researching and registering for fall activities, purchasing winter clothing when stores stock new sizes, planning holiday travel before prices increase, and scheduling annual medical appointments to occur during summer when school absences are not an issue. This anticipatory work prevents crises and optimizes resource allocation but remains invisible precisely because its success means future problems never materialize. Men, operating on shorter time horizons, address needs as they arise rather than preventing them from occurring, experiencing household management as responding to occasional demands rather than recognizing it as continuous future-oriented planning.

The time horizon disparity creates conflict when women's anticipatory concerns strike men as premature anxiety. A woman mentioning in February that summer camps require research and registration receives dismissal: "It's only February, we have plenty of time," indicating her partner has no awareness of registration deadlines, the research required to evaluate options, or the reduced availability and increased costs associated with late registration. His perception that "plenty of time" exists reflects his assumption that someone else (her) will eventually handle the research and logistics, allowing him the luxury of waiting until urgency finally penetrates his awareness. Meanwhile, she must choose between accepting the full burden of anticipatory planning or allowing preventable problems to develop to demonstrate that her timeline concerns were valid—a demonstration that often produces family stress she must then manage. The anticipatory time horizon also applies to household maintenance and replacement cycles: women notice that towels are becoming threadbare and proactively replace them during sales, that appliances are showing signs of impending failure and research replacements before emergency breakdown, and that children's developmental stages require preparing for new challenges before they arrive. This foresight prevents the household from perpetually operating in reactive crisis mode, yet generates no appreciation because, from male perspectives, needs are being addressed "too early" rather than recognizing that the apparent excess lead time is precisely what enables thoughtful, cost-effective solutions rather than expensive emergency responses.

The Mental Load in Professional Contexts

While the invisible load concept emerged from domestic labor analysis, similar dynamics operate in professional environments where women perform organizational maintenance work that enables colleagues to function effectively while remaining unrecognized and unrewarded. Women in offices notice when supplies are depleted and reorder them, track team deadlines and remind colleagues of upcoming obligations, facilitate communication across groups, remember birthdays and organize celebrations, maintain institutional knowledge about procedures and contacts, mediate interpersonal conflicts, and provide emotional support to stressed coworkers. This "office housework" parallels domestic labor: it is essential for smooth operations, largely invisible when performed well, disproportionately assigned to women through expectations rather than formal job descriptions, and typically unrewarded in compensation or promotion decisions. Research analyzing performance evaluations finds that women receive more recognition for communal contributions like helping others. In comparison, men receive more recognition for agentic contributions like individual achievement. Yet, the competencies valued for advancement correlate more strongly with agentic than communal behaviors, creating a double bind where women are expected to perform supportive labor that will not advance their careers.

The professional invisible load extends into what organizational researchers term "non-promotable tasks"—work that benefits the organization but does not enhance the individual's visibility or credentials for advancement. Women receive more requests to serve on committees, organize events, mentor junior staff, take notes during meetings, and handle administrative coordination—all time-intensive activities that divert energy from promotable work like publishing, securing clients, or leading high-visibility projects. Studies documenting committee assignments find that women serve on more committees than their male colleagues while also being asked to serve on additional committees more frequently than men, suggesting that organizations systematically extract more organizational citizenship behavior from women without equivalent career benefits. The parallel to domestic labor is precise: just as women maintain household infrastructure while men focus on career advancement, women in professional settings maintain organizational infrastructure while male colleagues focus on career-advancing activities, then those male colleagues advance more rapidly, reinforcing perceptions that they are more capable and deserving of promotion. When women attempt to refuse non-promotable tasks to protect time for promotable work, they face social penalties for violating expectations of female communal behavior, penalties that men do not face because male refusal to perform supportive labor aligns with expectations of male focus on advancement.

The cumulative effect of invisible labor across domestic and professional domains means women are perpetually operating at a higher cognitive load than their male peers, managing complex systems in multiple life domains simultaneously. At the same time, men focus their mental resources on single domains sequentially. A woman during her workday is not merely attending to her professional responsibilities but also monitoring school communications on her phone, coordinating evening logistics via text with partners or childcare providers, remembering to schedule appointments during breaks, and managing the cognitive switching costs of moving between work tasks and household management throughout the day. This cognitive fragmentation degrades performance in both domains: her professional output suffers from constant interruptions and divided attention. At the same time, her household management occurs in the interstitial moments of a workday already demanding full focus. Men whose partners absorb household management during work hours experience professional advantages that appear merit-based but actually reflect their freedom from the cognitive load that competing workers carry. The inequity compounds over careers: men advance faster partly because they can focus more completely on professional development, then their higher earnings justify their partners reducing work hours or assuming even more household responsibility, which further enhances male professional focus while constraining female professional growth, producing diverging career trajectories that began with invisible load disparity rather than ability differences.

The Weaponization of Incompetence and Learned Helplessness

Perhaps the most frustrating dimension of invisible load inequity is the way male incompetence at household management gets treated as an immutable trait rather than as a correctable skill deficit. Men who would never claim they are "just not good at" core competencies in their professional roles—project management, learning new systems, attention to detail, anticipating problems— suddenly discover they "just cannot keep track of" household schedules, are not good at remembering birthdays, or "do not think about" anticipatory planning. This selective incompetence reveals itself as strategic when examining which tasks men do competently track: men remember fantasy football deadlines, manage complex gaming achievements requiring extensive coordination, plan golf outings involving multiple participants, and maintain detailed knowledge of sports statistics spanning decades. The cognitive capabilities obviously exist; what differs is perceived responsibility. Tasks that men consider their domain receive full cognitive engagement. In contrast, household management tasks are treated as someone else's responsibility, requiring only compliance with assigned subtasks rather than ownership of systems-level awareness.

This dynamic creates impossible positions for women: if they continue compensating for male "incompetence," they enable and perpetuate it while exhausting themselves; if they refuse to pay and allow systems to fail, they typically bear the consequences more directly than their partners while facing blame for "not communicating clearly" what needed to happen. The weaponization operates through plausible deniability—men can genuinely claim they "forgot" or "did not realize" something needed doing because they have never built the cognitive infrastructure that would make them realize it. A man who has never maintained the mental model of when children need clothing in the next size genuinely does not notice his child's pants becoming too short, experiencing his partner's purchases as spontaneous shopping rather than systematic replacement of outgrown items. His ignorance is real, but it is cultivated ignorance maintained by refusing to develop awareness systems that would make the invisible labor visible. When women attempt to transfer responsibility by ceasing to perform anticipatory management, men often interpret the resulting friction as evidence that the management was unnecessary rather than recognizing that problems now visible were always being prevented. The child who arrives at school without required supplies demonstrates not that supply management is superfluous but that someone had been ensuring supplies were available and has now stopped—yet the man receiving calls from frustrated teachers often directs irritation at his partner for "not telling him" rather than recognizing his own failure to develop the awareness systems that would make telling unnecessary.

The invisible load will remain invisible until men develop the cognitive infrastructure to perceive it—not as discrete tasks requiring completion but as systems requiring continuous management, not as occasional demands but as permanent background processes, not as their partners' personality traits but as labor they could learn to share. This requires men to do something profoundly uncomfortable: deliberately cultivate awareness of domains they have been socially permitted to ignore, build mental models of household and relationship systems whose smooth functioning they have taken for granted, and accept that developing competence in these domains will initially feel overwhelming precisely because that overwhelm is the normal state their partners have been inhabiting constantly while making it look effortless. The path forward is not appreciating women more for invisible labor but rather making it visible by sharing it— actually building the calendar awareness, relationship knowledge, supply tracking, future planning, and systems thinking that currently exists almost exclusively in female cognitive space. Until men carry equivalent loads, they remain dependent adults whose partners function as combination project managers, executive assistants, and social coordinators, all while pretending the arrangement is an equal partnership rather than recognizing it as one adult managing another adult's life while also managing her own.

Chapter 11: Confronting Blind Spots: A Path to Genuine Connection

Men who sincerely want to understand women face a challenge more profound than learning new information: they must confront the parts of reality they have been systematically trained not to see. These blind spots are not random gaps in knowledge but rather organized zones of ignorance maintained through social privilege, defensive psychology, and the comfort of never having to examine how one's presence affects others. A blind spot in driving creates danger because the driver genuinely cannot see approaching vehicles; the peril lies not in malice but in the false confidence that comes from believing one's limited perspective constitutes complete awareness. Similarly, men navigate relationships with women while fundamentally unable to perceive significant dimensions of female experience—not because these dimensions are hidden, but because male socialization has installed perceptual filters that render certain realities literally invisible. The path to genuine connection requires not just acquiring new perspectives but confronting the disturbing fact that one's existing worldview has been incomplete in ways that have caused tangible harm. This confrontation demands something most men have been trained to avoid: the willingness to occupy uncertainty, to accept that they have been wrong about things they felt certain about, and to tolerate the discomfort of recognizing how their blindness has shaped every intimate relationship they have ever had.

The first blind spot men must confront is the illusion of meritocratic perception—the unexamined belief that they see situations objectively and evaluate people based on actual behavior rather than through interpretive frameworks shaped by gender expectations. Men routinely believe they are responding to what women do while remaining oblivious to how gender-based interpretation converts identical behaviors into opposite evaluations. A man who confidently labels himself an objective judge of character will describe a male colleague who forcefully advocates for his ideas as "strong" and "decisive," while describing a female colleague who advocates with equal force as "aggressive" or "abrasive." He experiences these as factual observations about different behavioral styles rather than recognizing that he is applying different interpretive frameworks to identical conduct based on the gender of the actor. This perceptual distortion extends across domains: women who negotiate salaries are "pushy" while men who negotiate are "knowing their worth"; women who express anger are "emotional" while men who express anger are "passionate"; women who maintain professional boundaries are "cold" while men with identical boundaries are "focused." The blind spot operates through a two-step cognitive process: first, the interpretation happens automatically and unconsciously, translating observed behavior through gender-based schemas; second, the mind presents this interpretation as direct perception of reality rather than as mediated judgment, creating the subjective experience of simply seeing what is there. Men cannot recognize this distortion from inside it because the entire system is designed to feel like an objective observation rather than a biased interpretation.

Confronting this blind spot requires men to develop what might be called "interpretive humility"—the recognition that their spontaneous readings of situations are not neutral perceptions but rather the products of specific socialization histories that have taught them what to notice, how to categorize it, and what significance to assign it. This confrontation becomes particularly uncomfortable when men realize they have been confidently wrong about things that deeply mattered: they dismissed a partner's concerns as "overreacting" that were actually accurate threat assessments based on information they never learned to perceive; they evaluated female colleagues as less competent based on behavioral differences that actually reflected gender-specific navigation of hostile professional environments; they interpreted women's communication as unclear or contradictory when it was in fact highly consistent once decoded through appropriate frameworks. The discomfort stems not just from being wrong but from recognizing that one's confident certainty was itself part of the problem—that the subjective experience of "just seeing things as they are" was actually the mechanism preventing accurate perception. Men must learn to treat their initial interpretations as hypotheses requiring verification rather than as direct observations of reality, introducing systematic doubt into mental processes that have always felt like simple perception. This is cognitively exhausting work that never ends; interpretive humility cannot be achieved once and then maintained effortlessly but must be practiced continuously against the constant gravitational pull toward believing one's perspective is objective.

The Projection Trap and Theory of Mind Failure

A second critical blind spot involves what psychologists call "theory of mind" limitations—the failure to recognize that other people possess internal experiences fundamentally different from one's own, rather than simply running slightly modified versions of one's own psychology. Men routinely project their own motivational structures, cognitive processes, and emotional topographies onto women, then experience confusion or frustration when women do not behave according to predictions derived from these projections. A man cannot imagine why his partner would be upset about something that would not bother him, so he concludes she is being irrational rather than recognizing that she has different priorities shaped by various life experiences. He cannot understand why she finds certain compliments offensive because he would be pleased to receive them, missing entirely that compliments carry different social meanings when directed at people occupying various positions in gender hierarchies. He struggles to comprehend why she experiences certain situations as threatening that he experiences as neutral, dismissing her assessment as paranoia rather than acknowledging that she possesses relevant experiential data he lacks. This projection trap creates systematic misunderstanding because it prevents men from asking the fundamental question: "What might this experience be like for someone whose life history, social position, and daily reality differ fundamentally from mine?"

The projection trap manifests with particular toxicity around sexuality, where men often assume women's sexual psychology mirrors their own with minor variations rather than potentially operating according to substantially different principles. A man might think that because he experiences visual stimuli as primary sexual triggers, his partner must respond similarly, leading him to invest in appearance-focused seduction strategies that entirely miss her actual arousal patterns. He might project his own relationship between sexual desire and romantic feelings, assuming that if she desires him sexually, she must therefore have romantic interest, or conversely that lack of spontaneous desire indicates lack of attraction rather than reflecting a responsive desire pattern that requires contextual activation. He might assume that what feels good to his body will feel good to hers, approaching sexual touch as though her neurological wiring simply mirrors his in slightly different anatomical locations rather than recognizing that entire maps of pleasure and sensation may be organized differently. These projections create sexual encounters where men believe they are being generous and attentive lovers while actually imposing their own sexual template onto partners whose needs they have never successfully perceived. The tragedy is not malice but the genuine belief that one is doing right while remaining systematically unable to perceive signals indicating otherwise.

Breaking the projection trap requires developing genuine curiosity about alien subjectivity—approaching one's partner not as a known entity whose reactions can be predicted based on one's own internal experience but as a person whose inner world must be actively explored and never fully known. This represents a fundamental shift from treating understanding as an achievement that can be completed to treating it as an ongoing practice that must be maintained. It means asking questions without believing one already knows the answers, listening to responses without immediately translating them into familiar frameworks, and accepting that some aspects of female experience will remain cognitively inaccessible to men, not because women are deliberately obscure but because certain realities can only be fully understood through lived experience. Men must develop comfort with permanent uncertainty about whether they are accurately perceiving their partners' internal states, replacing false confidence with appropriate epistemic modesty. This uncertainty is not weakness but rather the foundation for genuine intimacy, because real connection requires actually encountering another person rather than relating to one's projection of who they are.

Consequence Blindness and the Privilege of Ignorance

Perhaps the most consequential blind spot involves what might be termed "consequence blindness"—the inability to perceive how one's behavior affects others when those effects do not produce immediate, visible, or costly feedback. Men move through relationships creating impacts they never register because the costs of their actions fall primarily on women, who absorb those costs silently rather than generating conflict. A man interrupts his partner mid-sentence without noticing because she stops talking rather than fighting to finish her point; his experience is seamless conversation, while hers is repeated silencing. He makes commitments to domestic tasks, then fails to follow through without recognizing the downstream consequences because she simply handles whatever he neglected; his experience is occasional forgetfulness, while hers is having to maintain two separate tracking systems for what needs doing and whether he will actually do what he agreed to do. He expresses negative emotions through volume or intensity without perceiving how threatening this feels to a partner who cannot match his physical presence; his experience is honest emotional expression, while hers is calculating whether this situation might escalate into danger. Each of these impacts is real, substantial, and cumulative, yet remains invisible to him because the cost-bearing party has adapted rather than making the costs visible through confrontation.

Consequence blindness persists because male socialization teaches men that their internal experience constitutes the primary reality worth attending to—if they did not intend harm, if they do not feel they did anything wrong, if they can construct plausible justifications for their behavior, then no actual problem exists despite their partners' distress. This framework positions female emotional responses as data about women rather than as data about male behavior. If she is upset, the problem lies in her sensitivity rather than in what he did. Women's adaptation to this dynamic creates a feedback loop that reinforces male blindness: because women manage men's emotions by cushioning feedback and avoiding confrontation until situations become severe, men never develop accurate calibration about how their daily behaviors affect others. Their understanding of impact comes only from acute conflicts rather than from the continuous low-level signals women are constantly broadcasting, but men never learn to receive. When women finally do make costs visible through confrontation or relationship exit, men experience these as incomprehensible escalations that came "out of nowhere" rather than recognizing them as the culmination of hundreds of unregistered impacts that accumulated while they were not paying attention.

Confronting consequence blindness requires men to develop what might be called "impact consciousness"—systematic attention to how others respond to their presence and behavior, even when those responses do not rise to the level of explicit complaint. This means learning to read subtle cues of discomfort, withdrawal, or accommodation that women have learned to display precisely because direct expression has been ineffective or costly. It means tracking patterns over time: does she seem to avoid certain conversations, minimize her needs when he is stressed, or take over tasks he agreed to do? These patterns are not random but rather adaptive responses to impacts he is creating but not perceiving. Developing impact consciousness also requires actively soliciting information from a position of genuine openness rather than defensiveness: creating explicit opportunities for partners to describe experiences without fear of triggering defensive reactions, asking specific rather than general questions to elicit concrete examples rather than abstractions, and responding to difficult feedback with curiosity about one's impact rather than with immediate justification or contradiction. Most critically, impact consciousness means accepting that one's intentions do not erase one's effects—that meaning to be a good partner does not automatically make one a good partner, and that the harm one causes through ignorance is still harm requiring acknowledgment and repair even when it was not deliberately inflicted.

Jordan Ashford

The Epistemological Humility Requirement

Underlying all specific blind spots is a broader epistemological problem: men have been socialized to treat their perspective as neutral and objective while treating women's perspectives as subjective and biased. This creates an asymmetrical relationship to knowledge where men's observations constitute evidence while women's observations require external validation before being accepted as true. When a man and woman disagree about what happened in an interaction, most men instinctively privilege their own recollection as more reliable rather than recognizing that both parties experienced the interaction through interpretive frameworks shaped by different positions in social structures. When women describe experiences of bias or dismissal, men often demand evidence beyond women's testimony itself, as though lived experience does not constitute valid data. When women express intuitions or concerns based on subtle pattern recognition, men dismiss these as "feelings" rather than recognizing them as sophisticated data processing that integrates information men have not learned to perceive. This epistemological asymmetry means that women's knowledge about their own experiences and about gender dynamics is perpetually subject to male verification and approval. In contrast, men's knowledge is treated as self-evidently valid, requiring no external confirmation.

This blind spot operates at the level of what counts as knowledge itself: men have been trained to value explicit, articulated, evidence-backed claims while devaluing experiential knowledge, tacit understanding, and pattern recognition that cannot be easily verbalized. Women's expertise about navigating gendered worlds, about reading interpersonal dynamics, about managing emotional complexity—all domains where women have developed sophisticated capabilities through necessity—is discounted as non-knowledge because it does not conform to masculine epistemological standards. When a woman says "I don't trust him" about someone her partner wants to do business with, the man demands articulable reasons, specific red flags, and evidence that would stand up in court. Her response—"I can't point to anything specific, but something feels off"—is dismissed as insufficient even though her assessment may be integrating dozens of micro-signals below the threshold of conscious articulation into an accurate judgment. Months later, when the person proves untrustworthy in ways that confirm her initial assessment, the man experiences this as bad luck rather than as validation of her superior pattern recognition capabilities. He never updates his epistemological framework to grant her intuitions greater weight because his entire knowledge system is designed to discount precisely the forms of knowing at which women excel.

Confronting this blind spot requires men to fundamentally restructure their relationship to knowledge itself, accepting that their way of knowing is not the only valid way and that people whose life experiences differ from theirs may possess crucial insights they cannot independently verify. This means granting women presumptive credibility about their own experiences rather than requiring that every claim about sexism, dismissal, or discriminatory treatment be proven beyond a reasonable doubt. It means recognizing that "I haven't seen evidence of that" often translates to "I haven't learned to recognize what that looks like" rather than establishing that the phenomenon does not exist. It means accepting that women who have spent their entire lives navigating gender-conscious environments have developed expertise about those environments that exceeds men's understanding, regardless of men's general intelligence or education. Most uncomfortably, it means sitting with the possibility that one has been confidently wrong about fundamental aspects of reality because one's position of privilege meant one never had to develop certain forms of perception to remain safe, employed, or socially connected. This epistemological humility does not require abandoning critical thinking or accepting all claims uncritically. Still, it does require recognizing that one's own perception and analysis may be systematically limited in ways that are difficult to detect from inside those limitations.

The Collaborative Reconstruction of Shared Reality

The culminating challenge in confronting blind spots is learning to build shared understanding with partners whose perceptual worlds differ significantly from one's own. This cannot happen through either partner simply accepting the other's perspective as authoritative, nor through attempting to split the difference between two accounts as though truth always lies in the middle. Instead, it requires what might be called "collaborative sense-making"—joint investigation of experiences where both parties contribute observations from their different vantage points to construct a richer account than either could generate alone. A couple experiencing conflict about household labor cannot resolve the disagreement simply by counting hours or tallying tasks, because the invisible work that women disproportionately perform will not appear in such accounting. But neither can resolution come from the man simply accepting his partner's claim that she does more without understanding what she is actually doing, because sustainable change requires him to perceive the labor he has been missing. Collaborative sense-making would involve her explaining specific instances of anticipatory work, research labor, and relationship maintenance. At the same time, he attempts to genuinely see these processes rather than dismissing them as natural female tendencies or unnecessary work that could simply not be done.

This collaborative approach requires both parties to exit defensive postures and enter genuine curiosity about divergent perceptions of the same reality. For men, this means relinquishing the instinctive need to be right and instead becoming fascinated by the question of how two intelligent people can experience the same situation so differently. When a woman says she felt dismissed in a social interaction and the man insists no dismissal occurred, collaborative sense-making asks: what specific behaviors did she interpret as dismissal? What alternative explanation does he offer for those behaviors? Might his interpretation be shaped by not noticing subtle status cues that she has been trained to perceive? Could her interpretation reflect pattern recognition from similar past experiences, even if this particular instance was ambiguous? The goal is not determining who correctly perceived objective reality—often no such determination is possible—but rather understanding how each person's perceptual apparatus constructed the reality they experienced. This shared investigation builds intimacy precisely because it requires both parties to make themselves vulnerable: he must admit his perception may be systematically limited, she must accept that not all disagreements reflect his refusal to acknowledge her reality.

The practice of collaborative sense-making gradually erodes blind spots because it creates conditions where hidden aspects of reality can become visible through joint investigation. A man who approaches his partner's descriptions of microaggressions with genuine curiosity rather than defensive skepticism begins to notice patterns he previously missed: the slight tone shift when male colleagues speak over female colleagues, the different standards applied to male and female emotional expression, the systematic crediting of women's ideas to men who repeat them. These observations do not arise from being lectured about sexism but from learning to perceive reality through frameworks his partner has helped him develop. Over time, his perceptual world expands to include phenomena that were always there but that his prior socialization had trained him not to see. This is not indoctrination but rather the correction of induced blindness—learning to see what was occluded rather than having false information implanted. The deepest intimacy emerges not from perfect understanding or complete perceptual alignment, but from the shared practice of jointly investigating reality with humility about one's own limitations and curiosity about what one's partner perceives from their different position.

The path to genuine connection through confronting blind spots is neither quick nor comfortable. It requires men to surrender the false security of believing they already understand women and relationships, to tolerate extended periods of uncertainty where old frameworks have been revealed as inadequate but new ones remain incomplete, and to accept that they will make continued mistakes while learning to perceive what they have been missing. The alternative, however, is pseudo-connection built on male fantasy of who their partners are rather than genuine engagement with their actual personhood—relationships where men feel content while their partners feel perpetually unseen. Real intimacy requires mutual recognition, which in turn requires the ability to actually perceive the person one claims to love. For men, this means doing the difficult developmental work they were permitted to skip during adolescence: learning to see beyond their own perspective, to recognize how their presence affects others, and to understand that other people's realities are as valid and complex as their own. This work is not a favor to women but rather the prerequisite for the authentic connection that men claim to want but have been systematically prevented from achieving through socialization that taught them to mistake comfortable blindness for clear vision.

Chapter 12: Redefining Masculinity: Embracing Emotional Intelligence

The crisis of modern masculinity reveals itself not in the dramatic transformations society fears but in the quiet desperation of men who have followed every prescribed rule yet find themselves bewildered by the results. These men have accumulated professional success, maintained physical fitness, and learned to vocalize support for equality, yet their relationships remain hollow, their friendships shallow, and their inner lives barren. The missing element is not another strategy for optimization but rather emotional intelligence—a form of psychological sophistication that masculinity's architects deliberately excluded from the blueprint because its development requires precisely what traditional manhood forbids: the systematic cultivation of receptivity, interpersonal attunement, and comfort with states of not-knowing. Emotional intelligence is not an add-on feature that men can bolt onto existing masculine frameworks; it represents a fundamental reconstruction of how men relate to their own internal experience, how they process information about others, and how they conceptualize competence itself. This reconstruction threatens masculinity's foundational architecture because emotional intelligence develops through mechanisms masculinity has taught men to despise: asking for help, acknowledging uncertainty, prioritizing process over outcome, tolerating ambiguity without rushing to resolution, and valuing relational harmony as much as individual achievement. Men seeking to develop emotional intelligence discover they must dismantle much of what they were taught constituted strength, replacing reactive control with reflective awareness, defensive certainty with curious inquiry, and performative competence with genuine developmental humility.

The standard framing of emotional intelligence emphasizes individual skill acquisition—learning to identify feelings, regulate emotional responses, demonstrate empathy—as though these were neutral capabilities anyone might add to their repertoire through sufficient effort. This individualistic approach obscures how masculinity operates as an entire epistemic system that determines what counts as valid knowledge, which sources of information deserve attention, and what constitutes legitimate evidence. Traditional masculinity privileges empirical observation, logical analysis, and measurable outcomes while systematically devaluing or outright rejecting the forms of knowing that generate emotional intelligence: embodied sensation, relational intuition, affective resonance, and interpersonal feedback. Men are trained to trust what they can see, measure, and verify through replicable procedures while dismissing subjective experience as unreliable, feelings as distortions of reality, and interpersonal dynamics as too complex and variable to constitute actionable data. This creates an epistemological trap where the very evidence men would need to recognize their emotional intelligence deficits—feedback from intimate partners about relational impact, internal somatic signals indicating emotional overwhelm, awareness of interpersonal patterns that repeatedly produce disconnection—gets filtered out before it can register as significant information. A man whose partner tells him he seems disconnected might genuinely not know what she means because his attentional systems have been trained not to monitor for the internal states and relational qualities she is referencing. His confusion is not strategic avoidance but rather the predictable result of a perceptual apparatus calibrated to ignore entire dimensions of experience.

The Somatic Foundations of Emotional Awareness

Emotional intelligence begins not in the mind but in the body, through what neuroscientists studying interoception call "somatic literacy"—the capacity to detect, interpret, and utilize the continuous stream of sensory information arising from internal physiological states. Every emotion generates a distinct pattern of autonomic nervous system activation, muscle tension, respiratory change, and visceral sensation that occurs milliseconds before conscious awareness. People with high emotional intelligence have learned to detect these subtle bodily shifts and use them as data about their own state and about environmental conditions requiring response. A tightening in the chest might signal emerging anxiety, a warmth in the face might indicate embarrassment or anger, a heaviness in the limbs might reflect sadness or exhaustion, a quickening pulse might mark excitement or threat detection. These somatic markers provide early warning systems that allow emotionally intelligent individuals to recognize emotional states before they intensify into behavioral expressions, creating a temporal window for choice about how to respond rather than simply reacting automatically from within the emotion. Men, however, are systematically trained away from somatic awareness through cultural injunctions that frame bodily sensitivity as feminine weakness and through masculinity's demand for stoicism that requires ignoring physical discomfort, pushing through pain, and viewing the body as a machine to be commanded rather than a source of information to be consulted.

Research in psychophysiology using measures like heart rate variability—the natural fluctuation in intervals between heartbeats that indexes autonomic nervous system flexibility—demonstrates that men, on average, show lower baseline variability than women, indicating less flexible regulation between activation and recovery states. More significantly, studies tracking the development of interoceptive awareness find that boys begin childhood with somatic sensitivity comparable to girls but show progressive decline through adolescence as masculine socialization teaches them to override bodily signals indicating fear, discomfort, or need for help. Athletic programs reward boys for ignoring pain, fathers model emotional suppression through gritted teeth during injury, and peer groups police any sign of physical "softness" through mockery. By adulthood, many men have constructed what might be termed "somatic dissociation"—a habitual disconnection from bodily sensation except under conditions of extreme intensity. These men genuinely cannot answer the question "How are you feeling?" because they lack the interoceptive access that would provide an answer; their first conscious awareness of emotional states often arrives only when those states have intensified to the point of behavioral leakage through irritability, withdrawal, or explosive anger. Their partners experience them as emotionally illiterate, not because they refuse to discuss feelings, but because they have lost the somatic foundations that would make feeling-words correspond to identifiable internal experiences.

Developing somatic literacy requires men to relearn skills that masculinity trained them to abandon, a process that often feels like moving backward rather than forward because it involves becoming more sensitive rather than more controlled, more vulnerable to disruption rather than more resilient through suppression. Body-based practices—somatic therapy, mindfulness meditation focused on physical sensation, yoga that emphasizes internal awareness rather than achievement—provide structured containers for this relearning, creating permission to attend to bodily states without the immediate demand for action or resolution. Men discovering somatic awareness often report initial discomfort with what they find: chronic muscle tension they had normalized as baseline, shallow breathing patterns that restrict emotional range, or persistent low-level anxiety they had interpreted as simply their personality. The revelation that these are not fixed features but rather embodied consequences of years of self-suppression can be both liberating and overwhelming. Liberation comes from recognizing that change is possible; overwhelm comes from the cumulative recognition of how much psychological experience they have been missing, the emotional exhaustion that emerges when defensive suppression finally relaxes, and the relationship between their habitual somatic patterns and their interpersonal difficulties. A man who discovers he has been holding his jaw clenched and shoulders elevated for decades begins to recognize how this defensive armoring has shaped not just his physical comfort but his availability for emotional intimacy, his reactivity to perceived challenges, and his chronic sense of being under threat.

Affect Labeling and the Expansion of Emotional Vocabulary

Beyond somatic awareness lies the linguistic challenge of emotional granularity—the capacity to differentiate and name emotional states with precision rather than collapsing diverse experiences into crude categories. Psychological research on emotion differentiation demonstrates that people vary dramatically in the number of distinct emotional states they can reliably identify and label. Some individuals operate with a vocabulary of perhaps five to ten emotional categories—happy, sad, angry, afraid, surprised—forcing vastly different experiences into the same verbal containers. Others command vocabularies of fifty or more distinct states, differentiating not merely between anger and irritation but among frustration, resentment, indignation, exasperation, and offense, each describing a different configuration of circumstance, intensity, and response tendency. This granularity matters because emotional labels function as cognitive tools that make particular features of experience salient while obscuring others; the resolution of one's emotional vocabulary determines the resolution with which one can think about psychological experience. A man who can identify only that he is "upset" has little purchase for understanding what is happening internally or what responses might address it. A man who can distinguish whether he is disappointed, discouraged, defeated, or demoralized possesses dramatically more information about his state and therefore about what interventions might help.

Men typically operate with especially impoverished emotional vocabularies, a linguistic poverty that reflects both the cultural emphasis on emotional stoicism that makes subtle emotional differentiation unnecessary and the gender socialization that channels diverse male emotional experiences into the narrow acceptable range of anger and its variants. Studies examining gender differences in emotion words used in natural conversation find that women use approximately twice as many distinct emotion terms as men, with the gap especially pronounced for words describing vulnerability, interpersonal connection, and mixed or ambivalent states. Men show relative verbal fluency only for anger-related terms—frustrated, pissed off, furious, enraged— reflecting the cultural permission to express anger while experiencing pressure to convert other emotions into anger before expression. This channeling creates systematic distortion where men learn to label disappointment as anger, hurt as anger, fear as anger, and insecurity as anger, collapsing emotional diversity into a single socially acceptable pathway. The consequences reverberate through intimate relationships where female partners encounter male anger as the apparent response to everything, leading them to conclude their partners have anger management problems when the deeper issue is emotion translation failure: men are genuinely angry, but the anger is often a secondary response to primary emotions they lack both the somatic awareness to detect and the vocabulary to name.

Expanding emotional vocabulary requires deliberate practice with affect labeling—the exercise of pausing during emotional experiences to identify and name what one is feeling with increasing precision. This practice initially feels artificial and interrupt-driven, like stopping mid-conversation to consult a dictionary, because men have typically automated emotional responding without the intermediate step of conscious identification. The practice requires developing what psychologists call "meta-cognitive awareness"—the ability to observe one's own mental processes rather than simply being inside them—and maintaining enough emotional regulation that one can sustain curiosity about internal states even when those states are uncomfortable. Men beginning this practice often discover they have been misidentifying their emotions systematically: what they have called anger reveals itself as hurt underneath, what they called confidence was actually defensive compensation for insecurity, what they experienced as mere preference carried an intense emotional charge they had not recognized. Resources like emotion wheels—circular diagrams that organize hundreds of emotion words by category and intensity—provide scaffolding for this expansion, offering vocabulary that gives men language for experiences they have been having but could not name. The shift from "I feel bad" to "I feel inadequate and defensive" or from "I'm fine" to "I'm overwhelmed and need to withdraw temporarily to process" transforms not just communication with partners but men's relationships with their own experience, creating the possibility of responding to what they actually feel rather than to crude approximations.

Emotional Regulation Versus Emotional Suppression

Masculinity teaches men emotional management through suppression—the forcible inhibition of emotional awareness and

126

expression—and frames this suppression as strength, self-control, and maturity. Emotional intelligence, however, requires a fundamentally different relationship to emotional experience, one based on regulation rather than suppression. Regulation involves modulating the intensity, duration, and behavioral expression of emotions while maintaining awareness of their presence and information value; suppression consists of attempting to eliminate emotional experience through denial, distraction, or dissociation. The distinction is subtle but consequential: suppression treats emotions as problems to be solved through elimination, regulation treats them as information to be managed through skillful engagement. Suppression produces rigid emotional functioning where men oscillate between numbed disconnection and overwhelming floods when suppression fails; regulation produces flexible emotional functioning where men can experience full emotional ranges while maintaining behavioral choice about how and when to express what they feel. Suppression disconnects men from their own psychological reality and from authentic connection with others; regulation creates the possibility of being fully present to one's experience while remaining relational and responsive.

The neuroscience of emotion regulation reveals that suppression and regulation engage different neural pathways with different metabolic costs and different consequences for psychological and physical health. Suppression relies heavily on prefrontal inhibition—essentially using executive control networks to block emotional signals from reaching consciousness—which requires sustained metabolic expenditure, shows poor effectiveness over extended periods, and produces physiological stress even when phenomenologically successful. Men who suppress experience themselves as calm while their bodies remain in high arousal states, which cardiovascular monitoring reveals through elevated blood pressure, increased cortisol, and reduced heart rate variability. This mind-body disconnect accumulates health costs over decades, contributing to men's elevated rates of hypertension, cardiovascular disease, and sudden cardiac events that appear in seemingly healthy individuals with no conscious experience of stress. Regulation, by contrast, engages more distributed neural networks that include emotional appraisal systems in addition to control systems, allowing for emotional experiences to be reinterpreted or reframed rather than simply blocked. This cognitive reappraisal—finding new meanings in situations that change their emotional impact—produces more sustainable emotion modification with lower metabolic costs and without the physiological stress signature that suppression generates.

Men learning emotional regulation often resist the practice initially because regulation feels weaker than suppression; it involves acknowledging emotional vulnerability rather than transcending it, feeling emotions rather than overcoming them. This resistance reflects masculinity's foundational error: equating strength with invulnerability rather than with the capacity to remain functional across diverse states. Genuine emotional strength involves sustaining relational connection while experiencing difficult emotions, maintaining behavioral integrity when impulses urge otherwise, and returning to baseline after disruption rather than never being disrupted. Men who have built identities around stoic suppression experience the shift to active regulation as a loss of control because they discover they have been controlling themselves through rigidity rather than through flexibility, through avoidance rather than through engagement. The transition period can be genuinely difficult as men encounter the accumulated emotional backlog that suppression has been holding at bay: grief for losses never processed, anger at violations never acknowledged, fear about vulnerabilities never addressed. Partners often report that men seem to fall apart during this transition, becoming more emotionally volatile rather than less, as years of suppressed material surface. This temporary destabilization is not regression but rather the necessary disorganization that precedes genuine reorganization, the emotional equivalent of breaking a bone that healed incorrectly in order to set it properly.

Interpersonal Emotion Regulation and Co-Regulation

Emotional intelligence extends beyond individual emotion management into the interpersonal domain of co-regulation—the dyadic processes through which two people influence each other's emotional states through behavioral and physiological synchronization. Research using simultaneous physiological monitoring of couples during interaction reveals that partners' autonomic nervous systems become coupled during conversation, with heart rate, respiration, and skin conductance showing correlated patterns that reflect bidirectional emotional influence. People in healthy relationships co-regulate effectively, meaning each partner's regulatory capacity augments the other's: one partner's calm presence helps settle the other's activation, one partner's energy elevates the other's mood, and one partner's grief is held and witnessed by the other's stable presence. This interpersonal regulation creates what attachment theorists call a "secure base"—the felt sense that one's emotional experience will be met with appropriate responsiveness rather than rejection, escalation, or demands for immediate resolution. Men, however, often lack the interpersonal regulatory skills that make them effective co-regulators because masculinity has trained them to manage their own distress through isolation and suppression rather than through connection, leaving them without the experiential knowledge of how regulated presence can settle another person's dysregulation.

When women become emotionally activated, men face a co-regulation challenge they are typically unprepared to meet: remaining calm and present. At the same time, their partner is distressed without either shutting down the emotion or taking it personally. Men lacking co-regulation skills respond in predictable ways that amplify rather than settle their partners' distress: they become defensive ("Why are you angry at me?"), solution-focused ("Here's what you should do"), minimizing ("It's not that bad"), or avoidant ("I can't deal with this right now"). Each response prioritizes reducing the man's own discomfort at witnessing his partner's emotion rather than supporting her in processing that emotion, effectively abandoning her to regulate herself while her autonomic system is simultaneously activated by her own emotional content and by detecting his withdrawal. Women experiencing such failed co-regulation attempts describe feeling profoundly alone in their relationships, not because their partners are absent but because their partners' presence provides no regulatory support—indeed, often makes emotional processing more difficult by adding the burden of managing their reactivity while also managing their own emotional states.

Effective co-regulation requires men to develop what trauma therapists call "window of tolerance" expansion—the ability to remain in connection with others. In contrast, others experience emotional states that trigger discomfort in oneself. This involves learning to tolerate one's own emotional contagion responses (feeling anxious when one's partner is anxious, feeling sad when she is sad) without either blocking the contagion through dissociation or responding to one's own secondary distress rather than to her primary experience. Men must learn to distinguish "I feel uncomfortable witnessing your distress" from "Your distress is dangerous and must be stopped immediately," recognizing that discomfort with another's emotion is information about one's own regulation capacity, not evidence that the emotion is inappropriate or excessive. This distinction allows men to stay present through their partners' emotional processes, providing what therapist Bonnie Badenoch terms "presence that heals"—the regulated witnessing that communicates "I see you in this difficult experience and I am not leaving." Such presence requires no special skills beyond the willingness to remain, to breathe, to maintain eye contact, and to resist the urge to fix, argue, or flee. The power of regulated presence lies not in any action taken. Still, in the neurobiological signaling, it provides: the partner's calm autonomic state becomes available as an external regulatory resource that the distressed person's nervous system can use to settle.

Emotional Bidding and Relational Maintenance

The microsociology of intimacy operates through what psychologist John Gottman terms "emotional bids"—small gestures through which partners reach for connection, share internal experience, or request acknowledgment. These bids constitute the cellular structure of emotional intimacy: "Look at this sunset," "I had the strangest dream," "I'm worried about my mother," "Listen to this song," "Can you believe what happened at work?" Each bid represents a moment of vulnerability where one person opens a potential connection point and waits to see whether the partner will turn toward the bid (acknowledging and engaging), turn away (ignoring or minimal acknowledgment), or turn against (responding with hostility or criticism). Research tracking couples over years finds that relationship stability correlates powerfully with bid response rates: couples who remain together react positively to emotional bids approximately 86% of the time; couples who eventually divorce respond positively only about 33% of the time. The cumulative impact of thousands of bid responses or failures creates the emotional climate of the relationship—either a rich ecosystem of mutual recognition and responsiveness or an emotional desert where connection attempts wither from repeated neglect.

Men often fail to recognize emotional bids when they occur because the bids frequently take indirect forms that masculinity has not taught men to decode. A woman saying "I'm cold" while sitting with her partner on the couch might be making a bid for physical closeness (hoping he will offer to warm her), a bid for practical support (hoping he will adjust the thermostat or offer a blanket), or a bid for simple acknowledgment (hoping he will register her state). A man who responds "So put on a sweater" has technically addressed the content but missed the relational dimension entirely, turning away from the bid. His response focuses on problem-solving rather than connection because he has not learned to ask: "What is my partner reaching for in this moment?" The accumulation of such missed bids over months and years creates what women describe as "feeling invisible" or "living with a roommate rather than a partner"—their connection attempts are so routinely unmet that they eventually stop trying, producing the emotional withdrawal men often notice only when it has progressed to the point where repair becomes difficult. Men facing this withdrawal typically describe it as sudden and inexplicable:

"Everything was fine and then she just checked out." What they have missed is the hundreds or thousands of previous moments where she reached for connection and encountered emptiness, each failed bid diminishing her investment until reaching for him no longer feels worth the disappointment.

Developing emotional bid recognition requires men to cultivate what might be called "relational surveillance"—a background attentional process that monitors for connection opportunities rather than only processing explicit informational content. This means training oneself to notice not just what is being said but why it might be being said now, what emotional tone accompanies the content, and what response would honor the relational dimension rather than only addressing the topical dimension. When a partner shares a workplace frustration, the relationally aware response considers: Is she seeking advice (rare), validation of her feelings (common), or simply the experience of being heard and having her expertise witnessed (most common)? The default male response—jumping to solution mode—assumes the first when she typically needs the third, creating repeated experiences where she feels unheard despite his genuine efforts to help. Men learning bid recognition discover they have been systematically privileging information transfer over emotional connection, treating conversations as opportunities for problem-solving rather than as the relational glue that maintains intimacy. This realization often produces defensiveness: "Why doesn't she just tell me directly what she needs?" The answer is that she has been telling him directly, but in a relational language he has not learned to speak, and her repeated experiences of stating needs more explicitly have often resulted in him hearing criticism rather than invitation, producing withdrawal rather than engagement.

Integrative Masculinity and the Reconciliation of Strength with Sensitivity

The ultimate challenge of developing emotional intelligence involves not simply adding new skills to existing masculine frameworks but rather reconstructing masculinity itself around integrative principles that reconcile traditional masculine values—

agency, protection, provision, competence—with the emotional capacities that masculinity has historically excluded. This reconciliation requires rejecting the false dichotomy that frames strength and sensitivity as opposites, recognizing instead that genuine strength requires the full range of emotional capacities: the courage to be vulnerable, the resilience to remain present through discomfort, the integrity to align behavior with values even when emotions urge otherwise, and the wisdom to recognize which situations require firm boundaries versus receptive openness. Men attempting this integration face cultural headwinds that continue to mock male emotional expression as weakness, professional environments that reward emotional suppression as leadership, and internalized shame about neediness, uncertainty, or emotional overwhelm. The path forward lies not in abandoning masculine identity but in expanding its definition to include the full spectrum of human capacity, challenging the impoverished version that defines manhood through negation—not-feminine, not-emotional, not-vulnerable, not-dependent—rather than through positive articulation of what mature masculinity actively embodies.

This reconstructed masculinity recognizes emotional intelligence not as a concession to feminine demands but as essential competence for navigating an increasingly complex social world where success depends on collaboration, innovation, and adaptability—all capacities enhanced by emotional sophistication. The isolated, emotionally defended male who was functional in industrial economies organized around hierarchical authority and individual production becomes increasingly dysfunctional in information economies requiring network coordination, creative problem-solving, and cross-cultural communication. More fundamentally, emotional intelligence represents not merely a pragmatic advantage but the foundation for the intimate connections that men claim to want but have lacked the skills to build. The poignant irony of masculine emotional restriction is that it achieves the opposite of its intended effect: men suppress emotions to appear strong and thus worthy of love, but the suppression itself destroys the intimate knowing through which love becomes possible. Partners cannot love who men actually are when men refuse to reveal who they are; they can only love the performance, leaving men perpetually uncertain whether they are valued for themselves or for how successfully they hide themselves. The liberation men discover through emotional intelligence is not merely improved relationships with women but the possibility of being fully seen and still accepted, the relief of authentic presence after decades of defended performance, and the deep peace that comes from integration rather than division within oneself.

Chapter 13: Building Authentic Relationships: Mutual Respect and Growth

The architecture of authentic relationships operates according to principles fundamentally different from those governing transactional partnerships. Yet, most men approach relationships as they would approach any other domain requiring mastery: identifying objectives, developing strategies, optimizing outcomes, and measuring success through achievement metrics. This instrumental approach produces what might be called "performing partnership"—relationships that display the external markers of intimacy without the internal substance, where men execute behaviors associated with good partnership while remaining fundamentally unchanged by the relationship itself. The distinction between authentic and performative relationships reveals itself in how conflict is experienced: in performative relationships, disagreement threatens the structure because it exposes the gap between appearance and reality, while in authentic relationships, conflict provides information about evolving needs and emerging misalignments that require collaborative attention. Men conditioned to view relationships as problems to solve rather than ecosystems to inhabit struggle with the fundamental premise of authentic partnership: that the relationship is not an entity one maintains but rather a continuous process of mutual becoming in which both partners are perpetually transformed by sustained exposure to another consciousness. This transformation cannot be controlled, optimized, or managed into predetermined shapes; it requires surrender to uncertainty about who one will become through genuine encounter with another person's fullness. The terror this provokes in men socialized to maintain rigid self-definition explains why so many relationships stall at the threshold of authenticity—men reach the point where deeper intimacy would require them to change in ways they cannot predict or control. They unconsciously withdraw into the safety of a performative partnership where they can maintain the illusion of connection without risking genuine transformation.

Building authentic relationships demands what developmental psychologists call "differentiation"—the capacity to maintain a clear sense of self while remaining emotionally connected to another person whose needs, preferences, and worldview differ fundamentally from one's own. This represents perhaps the most difficult psychological work humans undertake because it requires holding two competing truths simultaneously: that one's partner is a separate person whose internal experience one cannot access directly, and that one remains profoundly affected by and responsible to that person despite the existential separation. Men often collapse differentiation in one of two directions: either they merge with their partners' emotional states, losing track of their own needs and boundaries in an attempt to maintain harmony, or they wall themselves off in defensive autonomy, insisting that their partners' distress is not their concern because they retain separate identities. Neither extreme constitutes genuine differentiation. Fusion produces relationships where men become chameleons, shape-shifting to match whatever they believe their partners want while accumulating resentment about their own unmet needs. This pattern often masquerades as selflessness or devotion but actually represents failure to develop a self robust enough to withstand the friction of difference. These men describe feeling lost in relationships, unable to identify their own preferences after years of automatically defaulting to their partners' desires. Yet, they simultaneously resist developing independent interests or perspectives because doing so might introduce conflict. The ironic result is that their attempts to preserve connection through fusion actually diminish intimacy because their partners find themselves in relationships with mirrors rather than with distinct persons capable of genuine encounter.

The opposite collapse into rigid autonomy produces men who treat relationships as optional add-ons to fundamentally independent lives—they have partners but refuse to be shaped by partnership, maintaining unilateral decision-making about major life choices while expecting their partners to accommodate whatever paths they choose. These men speak of "not losing themselves" in relationships, defending their separateness with a vigilance that reveals how fragile they experience their autonomy to be. They confuse differentiation with emotional invulnerability, believing that maintaining selfhood requires them to remain unaffected by their partners' needs or emotions. The anxiety underlying this defensive autonomy often traces to childhood experiences where dependency felt dangerous—perhaps because caregivers were unreliable, or because boyhood socialization punished any hint of need—creating adults who experience even healthy interdependence as threatening regression to childhood helplessness. Building authentic relationships requires these men to recognize that their defended autonomy is not actually a strength but rather a trauma response that prevents them from accessing the genuine security that emerges only through demonstrated capacity to depend on others and allow others to rely on them. The developmental paradox is that true autonomy—the ability to self-direct and maintain psychological integrity—actually strengthens through experiences of healthy dependence rather than through isolation. Men who have never allowed themselves to genuinely need another person have never tested whether their sense of self can withstand interdependence, leaving them with brittle autonomy that shatters under the normal demands of intimate partnership.

The Practice of Repair and the Rupture-Repair Cycle

Authentic relationships distinguish themselves not through the absence of conflict or rupture but through the presence of genuine repair processes that restore connection after inevitable breaches. Relationship scientists studying couples' interactions have identified that relationship satisfaction correlates not with conflict frequency but with repair effectiveness—the ability to recognize when the connection has been damaged, take ownership of one's contribution to the damage, and engage in restorative interaction that re-establishes trust and safety. Men often misunderstand repair as synonymous with apology, assuming that saying "I'm sorry" completes the repair process, when in fact apology represents only the initial acknowledgment phase of a much more complex sequence. Effective repair requires what might be termed "relational accountability"—the willingness to explore how one's behavior impacted one's partner independently of whether one intended that impact, to sit with the discomfort of having caused pain even when one's actions seemed justified from one's own perspective, and to engage in the cognitive work of understanding one's partner's experience well enough to avoid similar ruptures in the future. This proves extraordinarily difficult for men conditioned to defend their intentions rather than acknowledge their impacts, who experience any suggestion that they caused harm as an accusation of malicious intent requiring immediate rebuttal rather than as information about consequences they had not perceived.

The rupture-repair cycle functions as the mechanism through which relationships either deepen into greater intimacy or calcify into hostile distance. Each rupture—whether through overt conflict, subtle dismissal, or simple failure to meet a need—creates a moment of disconnection that threatens the relationship's security. How partners navigate this disconnection determines whether the relationship develops "earned security" that becomes more resilient with each successful repair, or accumulates what researcher John Gottman calls "negative sentiment override," where partners begin interpreting even neutral behaviors through lenses of hostility and mistrust. Men who lack repair skills often inadvertently train their partners that ruptures are permanent, that raising concerns produces defensiveness rather than reconnection, and that maintaining relationship stability requires minimizing needs to avoid conflicts that cannot be resolved. This training happens through repeated cycles where women attempt repair and men respond with justification, deflection, or counter-accusation, teaching women that the emotional risk of pursuing repair exceeds the benefit of potential reconnection. Over time, women stop initiating repair, not because the ruptures have stopped occurring but because they have learned that repair attempts predictably make things worse. Men in these relationships often express confusion that their partners seem to withdraw over "small things," missing entirely that these are not isolated incidents but rather the latest iterations of unrepaired ruptures that have accumulated into relationship-threatening damage.

Genuine repair requires men to develop tolerance for the vulnerability inherent in acknowledging wrongdoing without immediately defending or explaining themselves. The sequence matters: acknowledgment must precede explanation, and explanation must never function as a justification that implicitly denies the validity of one's partner's experience. A man who says, "I understand that when I stayed at the office instead of coming to your presentation, you felt like I didn't prioritize you, and I can see how my actions communicated that, regardless of my intentions," has completed acknowledgment. If he then adds, "There was a crisis with the client that I genuinely couldn't have predicted," he has moved to explanation, which is acceptable only after acknowledgment has been received and validated. If instead he says, "But you know how demanding this client is, so you should have understood that I might not make it," he has converted explanation into justification that invalidates the acknowledgment and prevents repair. The neurological challenge is that defensive reactions trigger automatically when men perceive criticism, activating threat-response systems before conscious processing can intervene. Building repair capacity requires training oneself to notice the defensive response as it arises, creating a pause before responding, and consciously choosing repair over defense even when every instinct urges self-protection. This pause—sometimes requiring men to physically remove themselves temporarily to regain executive function—transforms reactive defensiveness into responsive accountability.

Collaborative Growth and Developmental Asymmetry

Authentic relationships function as developmental contexts where both partners grow through their encounters with difference, yet this growth rarely proceeds symmetrically or simultaneously. At any given moment, one partner typically carries the growing edge—facing developmental challenges, struggling with new insights, or undergoing identity shifts—while the other provides stability and support. The relationship's health depends on whether partners can alternate these roles across time, each taking turns as the growing-edge person while the other holds steady, rather than solidifying into permanent configurations where one person perpetually develops while the other perpetually supports. Men socialized to view personal growth as weakness often resist entering growing-edge periods, particularly if those periods require them to be temporarily less competent, more uncertain, or more dependent than usual. They may support their partners' growth in abstract terms while subtly undermining it through emotional withdrawal during periods of disruption, increased demands for caretaking precisely when their partners have reduced capacity to provide it, or expressions of nostalgia for "how things used to be" that communicate preference for stability over development.

The concept of "developmental asymmetry" acknowledges that partners rarely need the same things at the same time. That relationship satisfaction depends less on perfect reciprocity than on trust that patterns will balance across longer time horizons. A woman navigating a career transition may need her partner to absorb more domestic labor and provide more emotional support than she can reciprocate in the moment, with an implicit understanding that roles will reverse when he faces his own developmental challenges. Men comfortable with this arrangement demonstrate what therapists call "secure base" functioning— providing stable support from which their partners can explore new territories without demanding immediate reciprocity. Men who struggle with asymmetry often keep what might be called "relational ledgers," tracking contributions and withdrawals to ensure they never fall into temporary deficit positions where they are giving more than they are receiving. This accounting mentality transforms relationships into zero-sum games where one person's growth necessarily comes at the other's expense, preventing the trust required for genuine collaboration. The irony is that men who refuse to support their partners during growth periods because it creates temporary asymmetry ultimately produce permanent asymmetry, where their partners learn they cannot depend on support during vulnerability and therefore stop sharing their developmental struggles, creating relationships where growth happens in isolation rather than through partnership.

Collaborative growth requires developing what organizational theorists call "learning orientation" rather than "performance orientation"—approaching challenges as opportunities to create new capacities rather than as tests of existing competence. Men with performance orientation experience their partners' feedback as evaluation that threatens their standing, making them defensive and resistant to change because change implicitly acknowledges previous inadequacy. Men with a learning orientation receive the same feedback as valuable information about how to develop capabilities they had not yet mastered, making them curious about their blind spots rather than defensive of them. This orientation shift proves difficult because masculine socialization rewards performance orientation through its emphasis on demonstrating competence rather than developing it, on never appearing uncertain rather than on moving through uncertainty toward mastery. Men must essentially unlearn the equation of growth with failure, replacing it with recognition that the ability to grow through feedback represents more sophisticated strength than the ability to defend against feedback through imperviousness. The relationship becomes a laboratory for this relearning. In this context, partners provide each other continuous information about how their behaviors land, what needs are being met or unmet, and where adjustments would enhance connection—but only if both partners approach this information as collaborative data rather than as performance reviews.

Negotiating Needs and the Architecture of Compromise

The pragmatic work of building authentic relationships requires developing sophisticated negotiation skills around the fundamental reality that partners possess genuinely incompatible needs that cannot be simultaneously satisfied. The romantic mythology that "the right person" will naturally want the same things obscures the truth that all intimate partnerships involve continuous negotiation between people whose desires, priorities, and preferences diverge in countless ways. Men often approach these negotiations from positions of unstated assumptions that their preferences represent neutral defaults from which their partners' preferences deviate, requiring justification or compromise. This asymmetry—where male preferences are treated as baseline and female preferences as special requests—corrupts the negotiation before it begins, ensuring that women bear disproportionate compromise burdens. Building authentic relationships requires men to recognize their own needs and preferences as equally particular and equally requiring justification as their partners', fundamentally reframing negotiation from "Why do you need this unusual thing?" to "We both need things; how do we create structures that honor both sets of needs across time?"

The architecture of fair compromise distinguishes between positions (the specific solutions people advocate for) and interests (the underlying needs those solutions are meant to satisfy). Men trained in positional bargaining—where each party stakes out an opening position and compromises meet in the middle—often produce outcomes where both partners feel resentful because neither person's underlying interests are actually met. A couple negotiating how to spend a weekend might engage in positional bargaining where he wants to go hiking and she wants to visit her family, "compromising" by doing half of each activity in a way that satisfies neither person's real interests. If instead they explore underlying interests—he needs physical activity and time in nature; she needs connection with people she loves and a break from her usual routines—they might discover solutions that meet both sets of interests more fully: perhaps hosting her family for a day hike, or splitting the weekend. Hence, each partner gets one full day devoted to their primary interest rather than two half-days where neither feels fulfilled. This interest-based negotiation requires partners to articulate what they actually need rather than defending predetermined solutions. This vulnerability proves difficult when people fear their needs will be dismissed as less important than their partners' needs.

The deepest negotiations in intimate relationships involve not just competing preferences but competing visions of what the relationship should be and who each partner should become within it. These identity-level negotiations rarely happen explicitly but rather unfold through thousands of small interactions where partners either support or constrain each other's emerging selves. A man whose partner is developing new interests that take her away from shared activities faces a choice between supporting her expansion even though it disrupts relationship routines, or subtly communicating that her development threatens him and should be curtailed. Neither option is cost-free: supporting her development requires him to tolerate increased separateness and find new ways to meet his connection needs; constraining her development preserves current patterns but communicates that the relationship requires her to remain static. Men who choose support despite discomfort build relationships that can accommodate continuous transformation; men who choose constraint build relationships that calcify around fixed identities that both partners may eventually experience as prisons. The negotiation is rarely explicit because making it explicit—"I need you to stop changing in ways that make me uncomfortable"—reveals its fundamental unfairness, yet the negotiation proceeds regardless, written into everyday interactions where enthusiasm for a partner's growth is either present or conspicuously absent.

Mutual Influence and Bidirectional Shaping

Authentic relationships involve genuine mutual influence where both partners shape each other's perspectives, values, and behavioral patterns through sustained interaction. This bidirectionality distinguishes partnership from pedagogy, where one person teaches and the other learns, or from accommodation, where one person remains fixed while the other adjusts. Men socialized to view influence as unidirectional—where they shape their environments rather than being shaped by them—often resist their partners' influence even when that influence would enhance their lives. Research examining couples' decision-making patterns finds that relationships where men accept influence from their female partners show significantly higher stability and satisfaction than relationships where men insist on maintaining final decision-making authority. The capacity to be influenced does not mean abandoning one's own perspective but rather remaining open to modification of that perspective through encounter with another consciousness that has access to information, experiences, and insights one lacks.

The resistance to mutual influence often manifests as what might be called "epistemic dominance"—the assumption that one's own knowledge and judgment are inherently more reliable than one's partner's. Men expressing epistemic dominance might dismiss their partners' concerns about people or situations because those concerns do not match their own assessments, insist on their own methods for completing tasks even when their partners' methods prove more effective, or explain subjects to their partners about which their partners actually possess more expertise. This dominance is particularly corrosive because it positions the man as the relationship's resident expert on reality itself, making his partner's divergent perceptions evidence of her confusion rather than data he should integrate. Building authentic relationships requires men to adopt what philosophers call "epistemic humility"—recognition that their own perspective is necessarily partial, that their partners have access to aspects of reality they do not perceive, and that integrating their partners' knowledge enlarges rather than threatens their understanding. This humility proves particularly difficult around subjects where men have been culturally granted presumed expertise, requiring them to recognize that their partner's lived experience as a woman provides her authoritative knowledge about women's experiences that his theorizing cannot match.

Mutual influence operates most powerfully not through explicit persuasion but through what psychologists call "relational modeling"—the process by which partners unconsciously absorb each other's emotional patterns, communication styles, and ways of approaching problems through repeated exposure and interaction. A man in a relationship with a woman who processes emotions by talking through them may gradually develop increased comfort with verbal emotional processing, while she may absorb some of his comfort with silence and internal reflection. This mutual shaping happens largely outside conscious awareness, making it critical that partners choose each other carefully—they are selecting the person whose patterns they will unconsciously internalize over decades. The question is not whether mutual influence will occur but rather whether partners recognize and intentionally cultivate the influence they want while resisting the influence they do not wish to. Men who remain unconscious of this process often wake up years into relationships, having adopted patterns they never explicitly chose, sometimes beneficial adaptations, but other times constrictions they absorbed from partners whose anxiety or rigidity became their own. Building authentic relationships requires bringing mutual influence into awareness, creating explicit conversations about which aspects of each other's functioning partners want to cultivate and which represent patterns they want to help each other outgrow rather than mutually reinforcing.

The ultimate expression of authentic relationship may be what philosopher Martin Buber termed "I-Thou" relating—moments where partners encounter each other not as objects to be known or problems to be solved but as irreducible subjects whose otherness is respected rather than domesticated into comfortable familiarity. These moments cannot be manufactured or maintained continuously; they arise spontaneously when both partners simultaneously release their agendas and defenses, allowing genuine encounter without predetermined destination. Men conditioned to constantly strategize and optimize often find I-Thou moments impossible to access because accessing them requires surrendering exactly the controlling orientation that feels like masculine competence. The practice is letting the relationship unfold according to its own logic rather than according to plans or expectations, trusting that a genuine encounter with another person's fullness ultimately produces better outcomes than carefully managing interactions toward predetermined ends. This trust requires faith in relationship as a developmental force more intelligent than individual planning—faith that remains difficult to cultivate for men trained to believe that security comes through control rather than through surrender to processes larger than themselves.

About The Author

Jordan Ashford is a relationship expert and author with over a decade of experience in social psychology and gender studies. Holding a master's degree in Applied Psychology from the University of California, Jordan has dedicated his career to exploring the intricacies of human relationships and the challenges that stem from traditional gender norms. Having facilitated workshops and spoken at conferences around the world, he specializes in fostering communication between genders, breaking down stereotypes, and promoting emotional intelligence. His passion for fostering understanding and connection in modern relationships fuels his writing, making him an authority on the often-unexplored dynamics between men and women. 'The Book On Women (For Men)' encapsulates his profound insights and practical advice, crafted for those ready to embrace change and deepen their connections.

About The Publisher

Welcome to The Book On Publishing

At The Book On Publishing, we believe in rewriting the rules of learning. Whether you're chasing your next big idea, building a better life, or simply curious about what should have been taught in school, you've come to the right place.

We're a platform built for dreamers, doers, and lifelong learners, offering bold, practical books and tools that empower you to take charge of your journey. From real-world skills to mindset mastery, we publish the book on what matters.

No fluff. No lectures. Just what you need to know, delivered with clarity, purpose, and a spark of curiosity.

Start exploring. Start growing. Start writing your story.

Read more at https://thebookon.ca.

Acknowledgment of AI Assistance

Portions of this book were developed with the support of AI. While every word has been carefully reviewed and refined by the author, AI served as a valuable tool for brainstorming, editing, and structuring ideas. Its assistance helped accelerate the creative process and clarify complex topics.

www.ingramcontent.com/pod-product-compliance
Lightning Source LLC
Chambersburg PA
CBHW060236030426
42335CB00014B/1478